Certification Manual

FDRP
Federation of Dining Room Professionals

ASSOCIATE HANDBOOK
CASUAL DINING STANDARDS

FDRP.com
Site Code CCI
P. 152

The Federation of Dining Room Professionals (FDRP)[®]

1417 Sadler Road #100
Fernandina Beach, Amelia Island, Florida 32034
USA

www.FDRP.com

904-491-6690

info@FDRP.com

Mr. Bernard M. Martinage, HGM, AHC, C.H.E.
Mrs. Cindy Martinage, DRA, WSA
Mr. David A. Swanson, DRM, AHE
Mr. Gil Kulers, DRA, WSA

Photographs by Mrs. Lorna Smith

Standards of Performance

The standards of performance for the techniques of service presented in this program are based on the IBGS of Hospitality, which is the:

International Business & Gourmet Standards of Hospitality

The Beverage Service Standards portion of this course, which is also included in the IBGS Standards, has received:

The International Sommelier Guild (ISG) Seal of Approval

The International Sommelier Guild is the only Sommelier certification body in the United States to be licensed by each State's Board of Higher Education for their 30+ satellite locations across North America.

An important part of the material used in this program is directly parallel to the *Certified Dining Room Apprentice* certification, which is a requirement in a growing number of culinary programs across the United States.

This program is endorsed by and is the recipient of the:

American Culinary Federation Foundation (ACFF)
Educational Assurance Award

Although the models photographed in this book wear uniforms often associated with the performance of service in a dining room of high standing, the techniques and principles exemplified apply to all full-service establishments--regardless of standing or style.

"There is a misconception that service is 'simple', but service is simple only when it is at its finest."

Cindy Martinage, Co-Founder, FDRP

 EXPRESS *Your Hospitality*®

Certified Hospitality Grand Master™

 Accredited Hospitality Coach™

Certified Dining Room Master™

 Accredited Hospitality Educator™

Certified Dining Room Professional™

Certified Dining Room Associate™
Certified Associate Wine Steward™

Certified Dining Room Apprentice™

Life Membership

Federation of Dining Room Professionals (FDRP)
1417 Sadler Road # 100
Fernandina Beach, Amelia Island, Florida 32034 - USA
tel 904-491/6690 - fax 904-491/6689 - www.FDRP.com - www.FrontSUMMIT.com

IV

Table of Contents

1 | Equipment Identification
Equipment Handling

This lesson you will learn how to:

- List tableware commonly found in contemporary dining rooms.

- Handle different kinds of glassware and flatware appropriately.

- Identify the proper way to handle a plate.

- Handle napkins appropriately.

- Identify the proper way to carry a Bar tray.

LESSON ONE

**Equipment Identification
Equipment Handling**

Objectives

By the end of this lesson, you should be able to...

- List the flatware commonly found in contemporary dining rooms.

- Differentiate the most commonly used plate sizes and their applications.

- Differentiate the most commonly used glasses, including an explanation of their ranging sizes and applications.

- Handle different kinds of glassware and flatware appropriately.

- Identify the proper way to handle a plate.

- Organize the storage of linen.

Equipment Identification

The three categories of equipment most commonly used to set up a tabletop are flatware, chinaware and glassware. Viewed collectively, the selections chosen by a restaurant establish a large portion of the dining room's look and service style.

Flatware

Figure 1-1 shows the most commonly found pieces of flatware in restaurants, including those used in formal dining, which is where specialty flatware are often used.

Overview of Flatware Uses

Demitasse Spoon: Espresso coffee

Bouillon Spoon: Consommé Cup
  (see Chinaware section)

Soup/Dessert (*Entremet*) Spoon:
  Soup bowl or appetizer / dessert plate

Sauce Spoon: Saucy items
  (not many restaurants have these)

Dinner or Service Spoon: Used to
  serve food items

Cocktail Fork: Used to eat small food
  items such as oysters and crabmeat

Salad / Soup / Dessert (*Entremet*) Forks:
  Put down with matching plate type

Fish Fork: Put down with fish dishes
  (not many restaurants have them)

Dinner Fork: Used with a dinner plate

B&B Knife (*Bread & Butter Knife*):
  Placed with a B&B plate

Salad / Appetizer / Dessert (*Entremet*) Knives:
  Put down with matching plate type

Fish Knife: Put down with fish dishes
  (paired with the Fish Fork and not
  commonly used)

Formal & Casual Steak Knife / Dinner Knife:
  Used with the dinner fork and dinner plate

A general overview of the basic flatware and its uses are presented in the 'Setting the Table' area of this manual. For a detailed description and demonstration of usage of all the flatware shown in the figure seen on the opposite page, please refer to the FDRP book, *The Professional Service Guide.*

Notes:

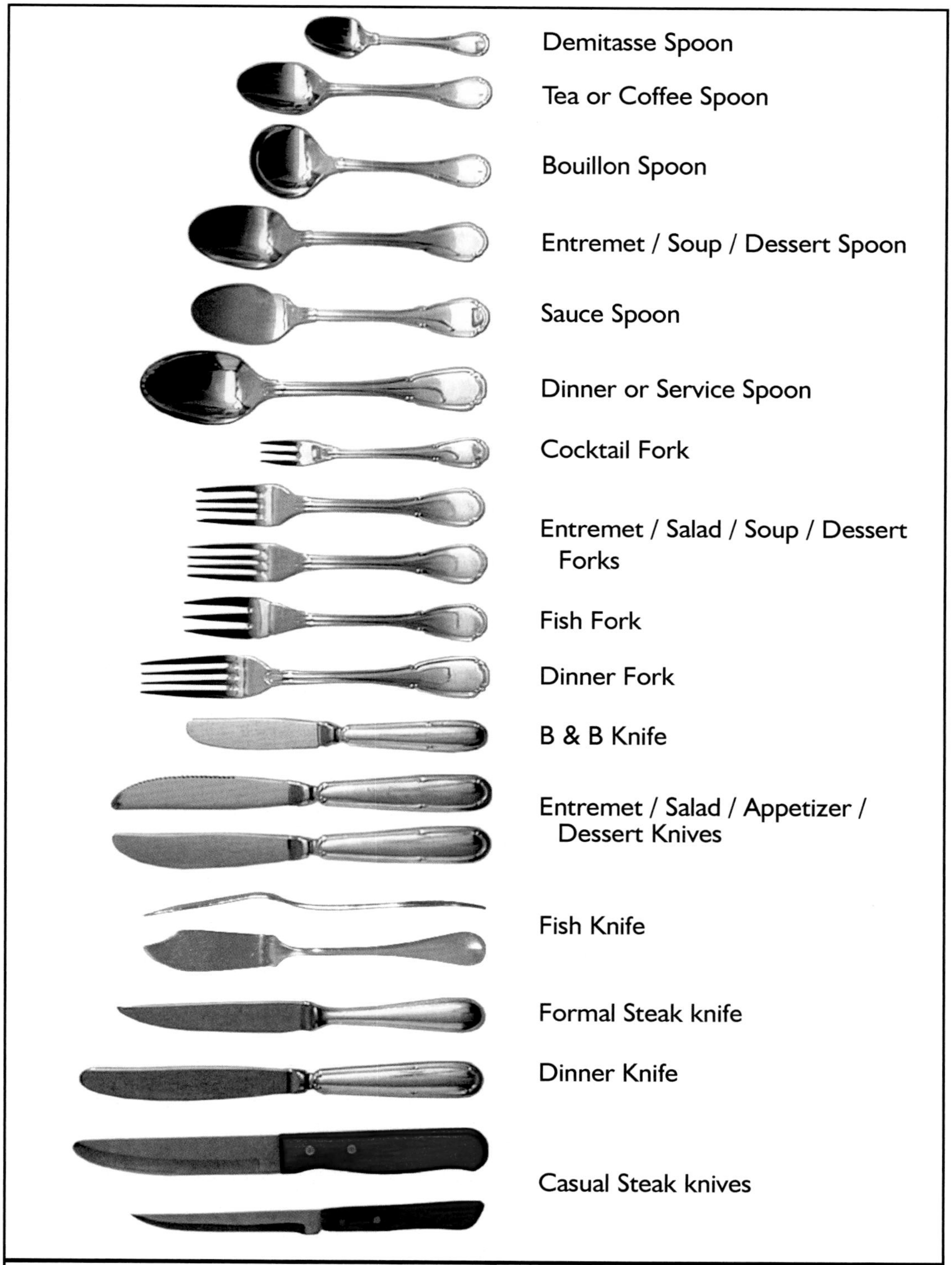

Demitasse Spoon

Tea or Coffee Spoon

Bouillon Spoon

Entremet / Soup / Dessert Spoon

Sauce Spoon

Dinner or Service Spoon

Cocktail Fork

Entremet / Salad / Soup / Dessert
  Forks

Fish Fork

Dinner Fork

B & B Knife

Entremet / Salad / Appetizer /
  Dessert Knives

Fish Knife

Formal Steak knife

Dinner Knife

Casual Steak knives

Figure 1-1: Flatware Identification

Chinaware

What makes up chinaware?
Chinaware can be made of many different materials such as porcelain, pottery, pyrex, ceramic, or glass. *Serving dishes of all shapes, sizes and materials used to present food to guests are also considered chinaware.*

Items such as:	Is there a special pattern or size?
- *Plates*	*No.*
- *Bowls*	*Most restaurants select patterns and sizes to fit*
- *Saucers*	*the types of food being offered. Color and styles*
- *Cups*	*can be eclectic to very formal.*
- *Vegetable and meat platters or bowls*	

Most plates are available in different sizes and patterns. *Vendors and trade professionals refer to a specific plate usually by its diameter in inches, such as "a twelve" for a 12-inch plate.*

The most common named plates are:

    Show Plate, also known as a *Charger* or *Base Plate:* Placed on tables *before* guests arrive. It is then either removed after the order is taken, or left on the table to be used as an underliner for appetizers, soups or salads. Plate sizes 'A' or 'B' of Figure 1-2 would be considered Show Plate options.

    The *Dinner Plate* (Figure 1-2, 'B' or 'C'): Used to serve the *main course or large dishes.* Its size can vary but usually is the *largest one*--unless the restaurant also uses Chargers, as mentioned above.

    Salad Plate, Appetizer Plate or Dessert Plate: Plate sizes 'C' & 'D' of Figure 1-2 would be considered Salad / Appetizer / Dessert plate choices. Some restaurants *also serve appetizers on smaller plates* (pictured by Plate 'E') and use 'C' or 'D' Plates for main courses.

    B&B Plate or *Bread and Butter Plate:* Used to hold the guest's bread and butter. *Placed on the left side of the place setup.* Can be slightly larger or smaller in size so it can also be used as a *Side* or *Garnish* plate for serving separate side dishes or starters. The 'G' Plate would likely be selected as a *B&B Plate.*

    The 'F' Plate will accommodate *Side Dishes.* Both 'F' & 'G' Plates could be interchangeable, depending on the restaurant's style and the size of other plates.

    Soup Bowl (Item 'H'): *Used for many types of soups / broths or food with a high liquid content.* Some restaurants may use a soup bowl to serve a specialty salad.

    Item 'I' is a Consommé Cup (shown with an actual *Consommé* serving): A *Consommé* is a flavored, clear broth with a light texture. It's served in a coffee cup-shaped dish with two handles.

Student task:

Write the names of each piece of chinaware in the space next to it.

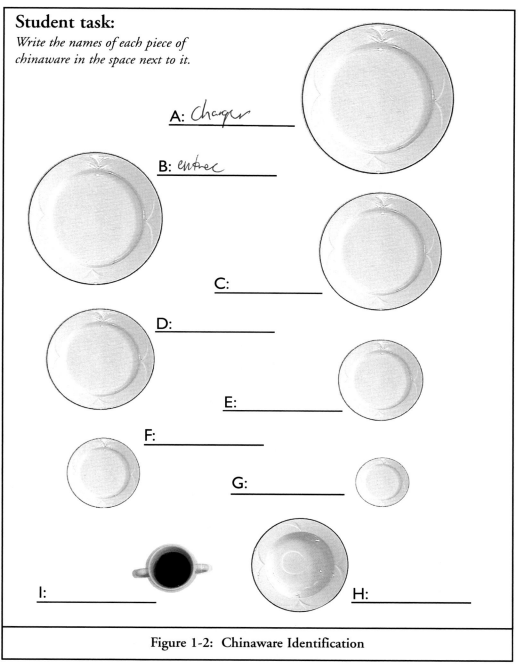

A: Charger

B: entree

C:

D:

E:

F:

G:

I:

H:

Figure 1-2: Chinaware Identification

Notes: 10:40 - done
V: resting

Glassware

What is stemware?

Stemware is another way of saying "wine glass" because it is used for serving a variety of wines. Examples of stemware's various shapes and sizes are shown in Figure 1-3.

Wine Glasses

Match the wine with the glass

- White and rosé wines are served in smaller glasses.
- Red wines, and water are served in the largest available glass.

Sometimes a restaurant will serve a *higher quality red wine* in a special set of glasses called *Degustation glasses or Tasting glasses.* The most well-known glasses with this designation are the *Bordeaux Degustation glass* (Type 'G', Figure 1-3) and the *Bourgogne (Burgundy) Degustation glass* (Type 'H', Figure 1-3).

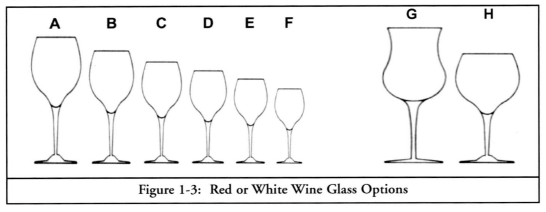

Figure 1-3: Red or White Wine Glass Options

The important guidelines to keep in mind when choosing glasses for service are:

1. *Red wines* usually benefit from breathing (receiving more air contact) and, therefore, should be poured in *larger and more "open" glasses.*
2. *White and Rosé wines are generally chilled* and should be served in *smaller glasses* to avoid the wine warming prior to its consumption.
3. Learn to use your eye for size. When looking at the glasses shown in Figure 1-3, if Size 'B' is used for white wine, then Size 'A' would be a good selection for serving red wines.
4. There are *very few glasses that are distinguished as either a white wine glass or a red wine glass.* Much of it depends on what the restaurant has selected for its glassware or stemware.

Notes:

Champagne / Sparkling Wine Glasses

Select a glass

Champagne and sparkling wines must be served in different glasses from other wines.

The Flute is the best shape of glass to help maintain the sparkling wine's bubbles longer (shown as Glass 'A' in Figure 1-4).

Glass 'B' is referred to as the Coupe. It may be more practical, but it doesn't preserve the effervescence very well.

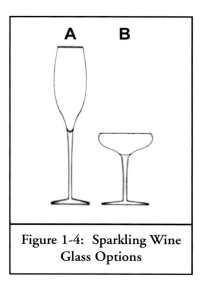

Figure 1-4: Sparkling Wine Glass Options

Fact: Different dining rooms will use different styles of glasses, but will maintain the size of glass appropriate for the type of wine being served.

Notes:

Equipment Handling

Correct ways to handle restaurant equipment will make a difference in how easily a server may provide the best service to guests. The more skilled servers become in handling the equipment, the more efficient and better prepared they are in providing the best service to dining room guests.

Glassware

Glass safety

Glassware is the equipment damaged most often in any restaurant because of its fragile and breakable nature.

What you need to know

It's always a good idea to keep one hand free while the other hand carries the glass. This way, the free hand can help the server:

- Keep others away from the glasses when passing.
- Provide a cushion if the server should fall.
- Stabilize the load if it becomes out of balance while being carried.

These guidelines hold true whether you are carrying all the glasses by hand or using a tray. The following information will help you learn how to handle glassware in the most sanitary, safe and efficient way.

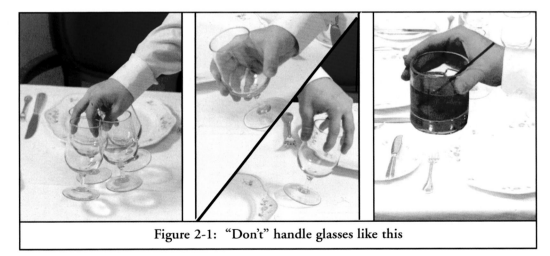

Figure 2-1: "Don't" handle glasses like this

Notes:

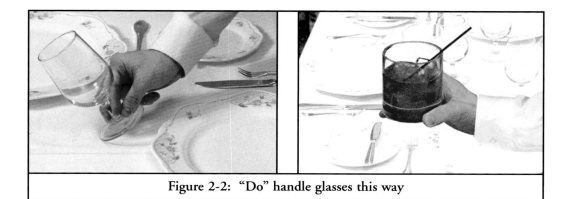
Figure 2-2: "Do" handle glasses this way

It's important to learn how to handle glasses safely. All glasses, with or without stems, should be handled in a way that minimizes skin contact. *Do this by holding the glass as far as possible from the rim.* This rule is true no matter how the glass is shaped.

The servers in Figures 2-2 *show the right way to hold a glass to minimize skin contact.*

When handling glasses made without stems, hold the glass between its base and midpoint.

When handling glasses that have stems, hold the glass by its stem.

These techniques:

- Maintain good balance, and
- Ensure sanitary conditions for the guest's lips.

Notes:

Carrying Glasses

There are two main ways to carry glasses:

    1. *With your hand* (seen in Figure 2-3).
    2. *On a tray.*

There are advantages to handling glasses by hand:

    1. Servers are able to move easily between seated guests.
    2. It decreases the risk of breakage, since there is no tray to balance.
    3. It is faster and easier for servers to take glasses directly from their station to the table.
    4. Servers touch the glasses less, thereby reducing the chance of leaving fingerprints.

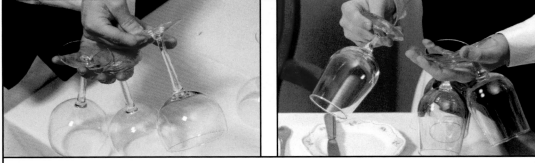

Figure 2-3: Proper methods of loading / unloading glasses by hand

Notes:

Figure 2-4: Preferred method of carrying glasses

Figure 2-5: Undesirable method of carrying glasses

Figure 2-4 and 2-5 show the difference between the server using his hands and using a tray to deliver glasses.

Holding glasses with the hand gives the server a more relaxed posture. *Notice how the server in Figure 2-4* can place the glass on the table without forcing the guest to move back.

Notice in Figure 2-5 how the tray has to be balanced while the server moves forward to place the glass on the table. That can be a very stiff and awkward position. ***If the glasses become unbalanced, the server runs the risk of dropping the glasses on the floor or table or even on a guest.***

Notes:

Chinaware

Carrying an Individual Plate

Chinaware will be handled according to the type of plate and its contents sent out of the kitchen by the chef. *Proper handling of plates is an important skill.*

Here are some guidelines that you will need to help you decide how best to present the plate to your guests.
- *Temperature of the plate.* Is it hot? Is it cold?
- *Style of food presentation.*
  - Is it covered with gravy that may spill over the edge?
  - Is it coated in powdered sugar that may leave fingerprints if you pick it up wrong?

These scenarios and others will help servers decide how best to handle the plates they serve. The following rules apply regardless of whether or not the plate temperature requires it to be carried with a "service-napkin."

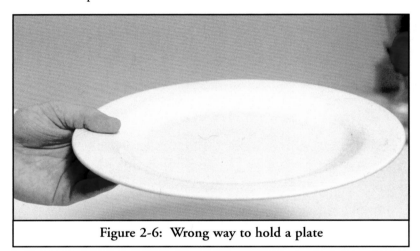

Figure 2-6: Wrong way to hold a plate

The incorrect way to handle a plate is to grab it by placing the thumb directly on the rim, shown in Figure 2-6. *This is wrong for several reasons:*
1. It doesn't make the plate easier to manage.
2. This technique will leave a thumbprint on the rim that guests will see.
3. If the plate is hot enough to require a service-napkin to hold it, the flap of the napkin will end up deeper in the plate than your thumb, possibly touching the food.
4. Skin contact inside the plate is unsanitary and can be a health hazard.

Notes:

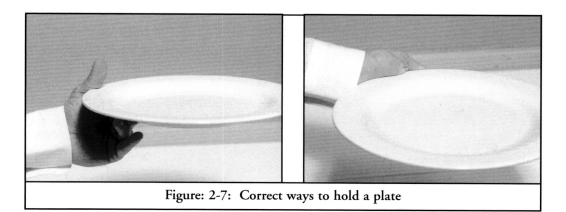

Figure: 2-7: Correct ways to hold a plate

Here's the right way to handle plates.

Figure 2-7 shows two different techniques to properly handle an individual plate. Notice that the server *never* places his thumb on the top of the plate.

The left photograph shows the technique that allows the most flexibility of the thumb position. This option allows the server to remove his/her fingers smoothly from beneath the plate, and *helps the server bring the plate to the table in a level, horizontal position.*

The left option can be awkward when using a service-napkin to protect the hand against a hot plate, however.

The second technique, seen in the right photograph, sets the server's hand in the ideal position *to place a perfectly horizontal plate on the table. Serving this way does allow more skin contact with the plate, but it still is considered sanitary.*

This second technique also works well if a service-napkin must be used, since the flap of the napkin is folded back over the top of the server's hand, thus hiding it and protecting it from hot plates.

Personal preference and comfort dictate how to choose between the two techniques.

Notes:

Carrying Multiple Plates

The rule of thumb is that servers really should not carry more than three (3) plates at a time from the kitchen to the table. **Why?**

> Because is looks awkward and increases the risk the plates will become unbalanced, causing the server to drop them.

Take one plate at a time to your guests if you are working in a more formal dining room. It's OK to take more than that if you're capable, and it's been approved by your dining room manager. <u>*There are three plate carrying techniques you should know.*</u>

Plate Technique 1

This is the easiest technique for stacking plates, and is practical for both serving and clearing plates because:

- This technique is strong and stable since nothing rests any farther up than the wrist.
- Servers can move the entire load freely without the risk of dropping a plate.
- The plates can be unloaded in any order since none of the plates rests on another.

With practice, the strain a server may feel in the hand when learning this technique will go away.

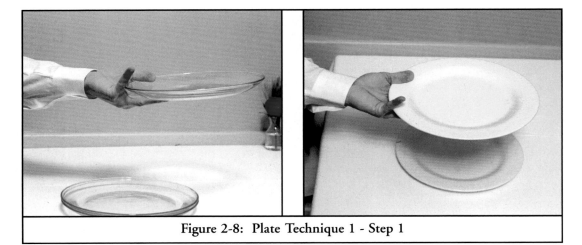

Figure 2-8: Plate Technique 1 - Step 1

The first plate to be placed in the hand is the middle one, which is called "The Stabilizer." This plate shapes the hand to support the additional plates.

Notes:

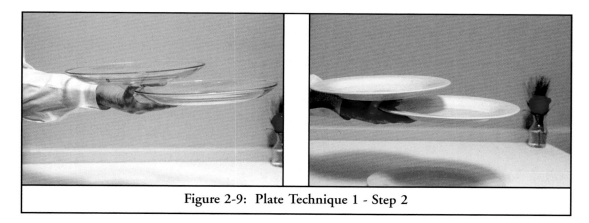

Figure 2-9: Plate Technique 1 - Step 2

Rest the second plate on the palm and pinky finger (Figure 2-9). Because this plate uses almost the entire hand, it is very stable and well balanced.

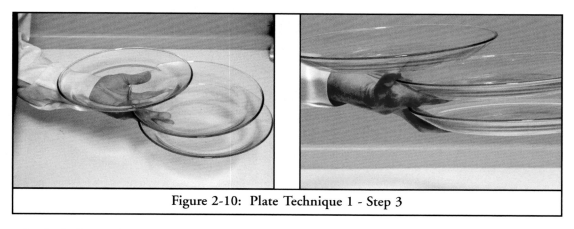

Figure 2-10: Plate Technique 1 - Step 3

The third plate is placed underneath the Stabilizer and held by the major (middle) finger.

The plate rests comfortably and is out of the way, directly under the other plates (Figure 2-10). A closer look shows the proper server finger position.

If a fourth plate must be carried, rest it on the top plate and the forearm.

Notes:

Plate Technique 2

This technique is a good option if the plates have tall or delicately-balanced food presentations.
Why?

> Because carrying plates this way allows the plates to remain level, reducing the risk of spilling the contents.

This method also lets a server plan ahead of time how to load them because the plates will be in _reverse_ order when they're placed on the table. **But...**

This technique requires a lot of practice and requires the server to always be aware of where the third plate position is on the arm in order to allow the elbow to be bent without any problem. *This method is not suited for clearing the table.*

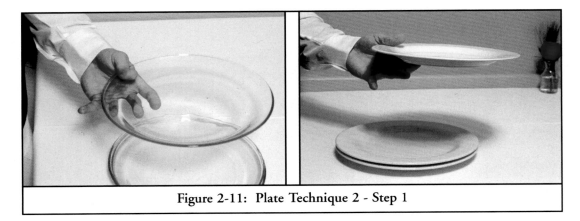

Figure 2-11: Plate Technique 2 - Step 1

The position of a server's fingers under the first plate are critical, since this plate is going to support the entire group.

The first plate must be perfectly placed in the hand, since there is no way to modify the position after loading the other two plates.

Notes:

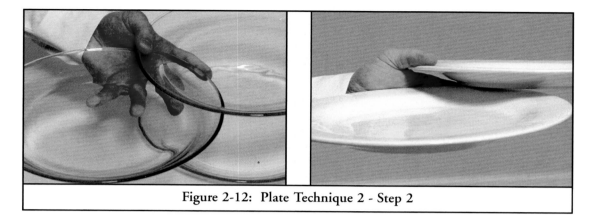

Figure 2-12: Plate Technique 2 - Step 2

The second plate must be placed in a way that the third plate can be securely placed on the second plate's rim. If food items protrude off of one side of the plate, point them away from the arm.

Be sure the plate position feels comfortable and strong before proceeding.

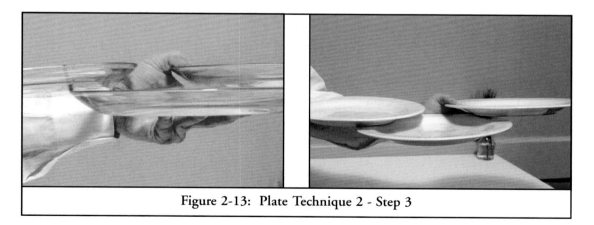

Figure 2-13: Plate Technique 2 - Step 3

Rest the third plate on the rim of the second plate and "lock" it in position with the forearm. Curl the wrist slightly inward in order to bring the second plate closer to the forearm. This increases the stability of the load.

Notes:

Plate Technique 3

This very popular technique is practiced industry-wide because it combines the best from the other two techniques. A server can unload the plates in any order *and* comfortably carry plates containing large amounts of food.

This technique requires a server to possess a strong hand since all the plates rest on the fingers.

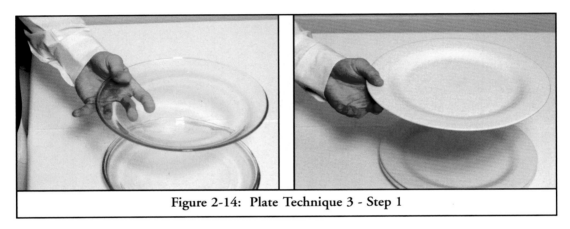

Figure 2-14: Plate Technique 3 - Step 1

The position of the first plate determines the server's comfort level with this technique.

Place the first plate on the first three fingers, ensuring they support more than the plate's rim. The server then has a choice of wrist positions, all of which are acceptable:

- *Straight*
- *Bent away from the body*
- *Angled toward the body*

Choose the position that is most comfortable to you.

Notes:

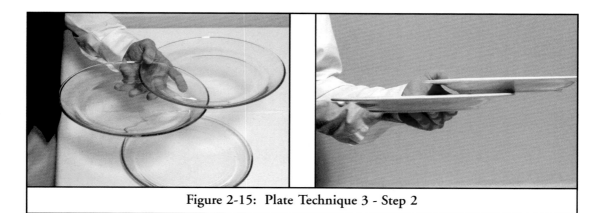

Figure 2-15: Plate Technique 3 - Step 2

The second plate is balanced on the pinky finger and thumb.
Once the second plate is in place check to make sure your hand feels strong and stable. This is important to avoid dining room disasters!

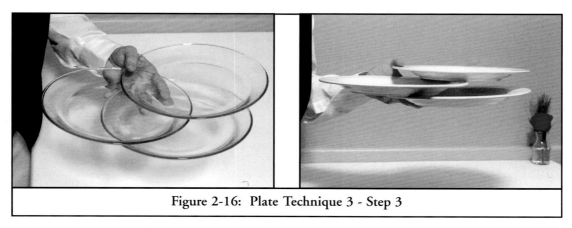

Figure 2-16: Plate Technique 3 - Step 3

The third plate is placed on bottom and is held by the middle finger. Utilize the entire finger length to secure this plate.

Any technique will feel awkward at first try, but will become second nature with practice.
Plate handling skills are as critical for a server as knife skills are for a cook. The rewards are:
- *Fewer trips to the kitchen*
- *Prevents spilling contents*
- *Overall better service to guests*

Notes:

Flatware

Storing

Since flatware does go directly from table to mouth, *the less skin contact you have with it - the better!*

Organizing flatware correctly helps prevent a server from being cut or poked.

Whenever an accident happens that draws blood, ensure all contaminated items are removed for cleaning and sterilization.

Organizing for Storage

Figure 2-17: Don't store like this

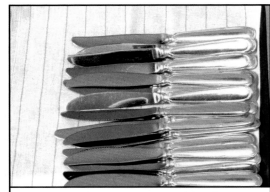

Figure 2-18: Do store like this

In Figure 2-17 the knives are pointing in different directions. This can lead to:

- A cut
- Smudging the blades of knives by picking them up

Figure 2-18 shows a simple and practical way to store knives in a side stand.

*Knives are placed in the same direction **with all the blades facing down.** This method is easy, clean, plus fast to stock and use.*

Notes:

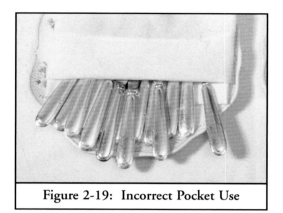

Figure 2-19: Incorrect Pocket Use

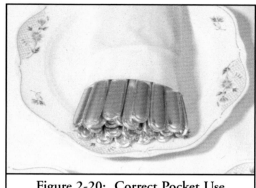

Figure 2-20: Correct Pocket Use

Napkin pockets are great if knives are stored somewhere other than a drawer or side stand.

- *Wrap the napkin pocket tightly around the flatware to prevent spilling on the floor.*
- *Make sure it's not too loose,* like the one shown in Figure 2-19.

Figure 2-20 is the correct use of the pocket.
Flatware can also be placed on top of a napkin, as long as all the flatware points the same way.

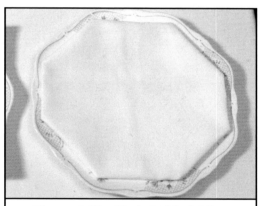

Figure: 2-21: Undesirable folding

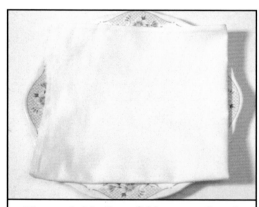

Figure: 2-22: Less folds are preferred

If an establishment uses Service Transport Plates (STP), flatware is placed on top of a napkin and the entire plate is taken to the table. Keep napkin folding simple, as in Figure 2-22.

Notes:

Handling at the Table

As a server, you will handle flatware two ways:

1. Organizing it to take to the table, and
2. Presenting it to the guests you're serving.

Goal: To place the flatware down on the table without disrupting your guests.

Use a napkin on the STP to cut back on noise and minimize skin contact.

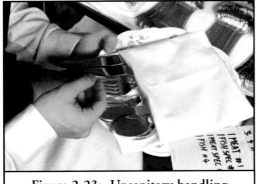

Figure 2-23: Unsanitary handling

Figure: 2-24: Which flatware do I pull?

Don't carry flatware as pictured above.

In Figure 2-23, the server ends up touching the fork tines or knife blades - unsanitary!

In Figure 2-24, the server has to pull out a piece of flatware from the napkin before he can tell if it is a fork or a knife - not efficient!

Notes:

Figure 2-25: Grouping by category

Figure 2-26: Grouping by guest

There are two different methods to organize the flatware on a STP:

1. *By category* (Figure 2-25): The waiter groups (or assembles) the sets at the table according to what the guests ordered.
2. *By guest / setting* (Figure 2-26): The waiter pre-groups the flatware on the STP in guest placement order.

The STP organization method depends on:

1. *The complexity of the set up*   and   2. *The number of people in the party*

When placing a table *(also sometimes called Tooling or Marking)* for a large party, pre-grouping by guest may not be possible on a single plate. *Grouping by guest generally works smoothly for less than six guests.*

Figure 2-27: Assembling flatware

Figure 2-28: Flatware tray brought to table

Figure 2-27 demonstrates a server grouping flatware from the STP at the guest table. Another way to use the STP is to have trays pre-set with flatware sorted by type (Figure 2-28). The entire tray is often taken to the table along with the documentation corresponding to that order or course.

Notes:

Rules for flatware placement

These rules apply regardless of the type of dining room or style of service:

1. Flatware should be placed on the table *BEFORE* the food is brought to the table.

2. Do not touch any part of the flatware that will come into contact with food, if at all possible.

3. Right hand lays down flatware on the right side of the guest and vice versa.
   This avoids elbowing the guest!

4. Avoid reaching across the table.

5. *If you lay down the wrong flatware, make the change as quickly as you notice it--hopefully before the food is served. If in question, consider if the food is already served. The server must decide:*
   A. If the flatware can be used to eat the dish, even though it is not the desired utensil or an accessory is missing (such as a sauce spoon), then do not correct the flatware.
   B. If the flatware cannot be used to eat the dish, e.g. a fish knife was given instead of a steak knife, always correct the error immediately.

6. *If a guest does not move out of the way for you to set the flatware down, consider the following:*
   A. *The guest is talking. If the guest is in the same position after taking care of the other guests, place the flatware down on whatever side is available.* Either the guest will take care of it or you can come back later to make adjustments.
   B. *The guest is not talking. Excuse yourself and present the flatware.* If the guest moves out of the way, set the flatware down. If the guest ignores you, place the flatware down on whatever side is available. Either the guest will take care of it or you can come back later to make adjustments.

7. *If a guest hands you an item and says it's dirty, provide a clean utensil promptly.*

8. If a guest drops an item on the floor, replace it promptly.

9. If a guest requests an extra piece of silverware that is not appropriate for the dish, bring the guest whatever they asked for!

10. If you see a guest sliding an item in his/her pocket or purse with the obvious intent to to take it, contact your manager and let him/her deal with it.

Notes:

Figure 2-29: Grouping at the table

It is preferable to place flatware with your right hand from the guest's right side (Figure 2-29) and/or with the left hand from the guest's left side.

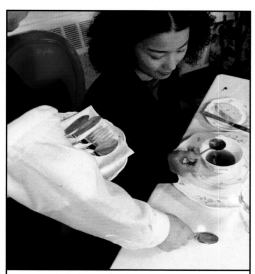

Figure 2-30: Bad time to place flatware

Figure 2-31: Good time to place flatware

Do not place flatware for the next course while guests are eating or have food from the current course in front of them.

Wait until the table is free from activity (seen above in Figure 2-31).

Notes:

Napkin Standards

Skin contact should always be minimized with any item that a guest might either consume or could touch their mouth or face with during use. Napkins are one of the few items that are in almost constant contact with a guest. From a server's viewpoint, napkins are handled outside set up:

1. Immediately following the guest's initial seating, and
2. After the guest momentarily leaves the table.

At Seating

Handling of the napkin after set up should be left to the guest.

Some servers believe that unfolding a guest's napkin and putting it on their lap (Figure 1-1) provides a higher level of service. Not so! It is rude for guests to unfold their napkin if not everyone has arrived. So unfolding the napkin for a guest may violate the rules of etiquette.

Don't help guests with their napkins unless you are asked to assist them.

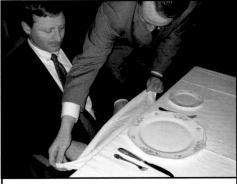

Figure 1-1: Inappropriate Napkin Help

Servers may need to ask guests to remove a napkin from a water glass. Some restaurants place a folded napkin inside the glass. If this is the case, politely ask the guest to remove the napkin from the glass. This ensures the napkin will remain sanitary.

During the Meal

A server may need to replace the guest's napkin if:

- It falls on the floor, or
- A guest leaves the table momentarily and drops it into the seat or on the floor.

The correct procedure to follow every time a server handles a customer's used napkin is:

1. Provide the customer with a fresh napkin.
2. Put the used napkin in the dirty linen bag.
3. Wash hands.

Rule of thumb:
The guest is never without a napkin, and clean napkins are always handled with clean hands.

Notes:

Keep Linens Sanitary

A napkin is always replaced if it falls on the floor. If the napkin is on the table next to the guest's set up, no replacement is necessary.

Many guests leave napkins on the seat of the chair. It is IDEAL to bring a fresh napkin to prevent a guest from using a napkin that has been on a seat where countless other guests have sat. It's OK to leave the napkin where the guest has left it unless it falls on the floor.

It is the responsibility of the dining room staff to keep a watchful eye on guests who temporarily leave the table. Again, when in doubt, always take the sanitary route!

A server should never refold a used napkin and put it back on the table or leave a re-folded napkin on the chair's armrest (see Figure 2-33). **Why?** It violates all rules of sanitation. The napkin is now contaminated not only by the table or arm rest, but now the server has touched it and has contaminated it even more.

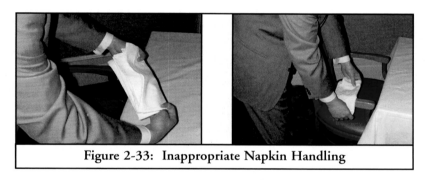

Figure 2-33: Inappropriate Napkin Handling

Always replace a contaminated napkin with a fresh one (Figure 2-34).

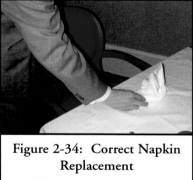

Figure 2-34: Correct Napkin Replacement

Notes:

Linen

In the dining room, napkins and tablecloths fall into this category. Typically, cleaning companies are employed to clean, press and fold linen.

When preparing linen, the most important guideline is to handle it as little as possible. When styling a napkin, reducing the number of required folds reduces skin contact with the napkin and is very desirable.

Always remember! It is unsanitary to reuse linen that has been in contact with guests, whether tablecloths or napkins. Servers should also wash their hands after handling dirty linen.

When storing stacks of linen, whether it is on a shelf or in a cupboard, follow these two universal rules:

1. *Place the fresh linen underneath the existing stacked linen.* This technique avoids using the same linen over and over, thus wearing it out. White linen that remains unused also has a tendency to turn yellow in color or become heavily wrinkled.
2. *Linen should be stored in such a way that the folded side is exposed* (Figure 2-35) for easy selection. If the open side (Figure 2-36) is exposed, the linen tends to unfold in the server's hand as it is picked up, requiring the server to refold it and lose time.

When setting a table with a tablecloth follow these six universal rules:

1. For large tables, overlap tablecloths like shingles starting from the opposite end of the entrance to the room. This makes the overlap almost invisible.
2. Place tablecloths hemmed-side down.
3. Align corners with the table's legs (when possible).
4. Overlaid tablecloths should line up corner-to-corner with the one below.
5. Align the center crease with the center of the table.
6. The center crease must be pointing upward.

Figure 2-35: Correct way to store linen

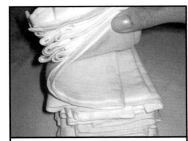

Figure: 2-36: Wrong way to store linen

During service, it is not uncommon for a guest to need a napkin replacement. A restaurant with a good sanitation policy stocks the dining room with ample fresh linen.

Notes:

Trays

Trays come in a variety of sizes and fulfill a variety of service needs.

Trays fall into three categories:

1. *Bar trays (generally used for multiple drinks and small loads).*
2. *Food trays (generally used for plates and large loads).*
3. *Hand/cocktail trays (generally used for a single drink and small items such as the check).*

It is common for one restaurant to use all three types of trays.

The basics of *tray loading* and *tray carrying* techniques shown here improve the speed, safety, and elegance of service.

How well the tray is handled has a positive effect on sales, breakage reduction, and also improves the professional look of the service.

Proper tray handling also includes anticipating problems while carrying the tray. You must:

- *Know the permitted paths* and your options if an obstacle presents itself.
- *Know where and how the tray will be put down.*

Never carry more than what is comfortable! A server must feel strong at all times.

Rules of thumb:

- *Keep one hand available, if possible.*
- *Never run with a tray.*
- *Always check to see if the forward path is clear of obstacles or wet spots.*
- *Be aware that anyone, even a guest, may back up on you.*
- *Make your presence known by either putting up a hand or elbow, or excuse yourself by progressively raising your voice.*
- *Heavy items should not be placed at the center of the tray, but instead placed towards your body in order to make the tray easier to carry.*

Notes:

Bar Tray

The bar tray is medium-sized and comes in a variety of shapes.

This tray type is the one most often used around guests. Servers use this tray to:

- Deliver drinks, including coffee and tea
- Transport clean glasses in the dining room
- Clear a few items from a guest's table

Proper handling of a bar tray begins with selecting the correct hand position with which to carry the tray.

| Figure 2-37: Don't hold a tray this way | Figure 2-38: Don't hold a tray like this |

Even though the technique presented in Figure 2-37 is pleasing to the eye and widely used, it is not a good way to hold the tray. That is because the server will shake the tray, and all the items on it, with each step.

Carrying a bar tray with both hands, as shown in Figure 2-38, is a safety hazard for both the server and others. **Why?** Using a tray this way increases the difficulty to avoid trouble spots on the floor or stairs. Maintaining a free hand allows a server to:

- Avoid collisions;
- Maintain (or regain) balance; and
- Unload the tray without setting it down.

Notes:

Figure 2-39 shows the proper way to place your hand under a tray. The entire hand supports the weight of the tray, increasing balance and strength.

Notice that the tray does not rest on any other part of the body. This increases the server's speed and tray movement options <u>and</u> *the server's other hand remains available for use.*

This technique is used regardless of the tray's shape.

Figure 2-39: Good hand position

Figure 2-40 demonstrates the most efficient and appropriate way to handle a tray around a table.

Hold the tray in your hand and go around the table, loading or clearing discreetly.

Do not *clear more than one table at a time with the same tray in the presence of guests.*

Do not *put the tray down on the table.*

Figure 2-40: Proper tray handling

Notes:

2 | Setting the Table
Styles of Service & Clearing

In this lesson you will learn how to:

- **Perform Modern set up of a table.**

- **Set a table for a banquet.**

- **Perform proper American Service (Individual Plate Service).**

- **Identify other classic service styles.**

LESSON TWO

Setting the Table, Styles of Service & Clearing

Objectives

By the end of this lesson, you should be able to…

- Describe the difference between Modern and Modern Casual table set up.

- Set a table ready for a Banquet.

- Execute American Service (Individual Plate Service) according the standard demonstrated by the mentor.

- Discretely clear a table of used dishes and flatware.

Setting the Table

The demands and expectations of today's guests are very different from what they were just a few years ago. Service is a constantly evolving art form that requires a consistent focus on the guest, a great aesthetic sense, and a strategic mind to execute within the tight parameters of time and profit.

Today, there exist a number of interpretations of the most popular set up styles. In this section, three standard settings are presented.

"A la carte" Setting: Modern Set Up

"A la carte" implies that guests will choose the food for their meal after they are seated. *There are two models that can be followed in the "a la carte" set up:*

1. The *Traditional*, or *Classic Gastronomique, which is not included in this course.*
2. The *Modern* or *Basic, which is one of the most common settings used today.*

The Modern set up presented here is the easiest. This very common set up is what most people expect to see on a dining room table upon seating. The modern set up is found in a wide variety of establishments, from casual to semi-formal and even some formal dining rooms.

Figure 3-1: Modern Set Up Examples

Notes:

The Modern set ups shown in Figure 5-1 each contains:

    a. One plate, typically the Show plate (also referred to as a 'charger')
    b. One napkin
    c. One B&B knife (bread-and-butter knife)
    d. One B&B plate (bread-and-butter plate)
    e. One fork
    f. One knife
    g. An optional glass

In set ups that involve a show plate (charger) it is critical to *detail* the show plate first since the entire set up will be adjusted to the location of this plate. It can only be correctly performed if the server stands directly behind the setting.

In the Modern set up, the B&B knife is consistently placed on the right side of the B&B plate, with the blade facing the left. This allows the guests to use the knife without rotating it in their hand. Some establishments place the knife horizontally across the top of the B&B plate, which is also considered correct.

If the flatware is main course size, the server will only have to add the necessary flatware for the appetizers and have nothing to add for the main course unless the guest uses the wrong utensils.

If the flatware is of the appetizer type, the server will not have to touch anything until setting for the main course unless the guest orders a soup or an appetizer that requires a special utensil.

Another addition to this set up is a glass. Water is usually offered to guest without request, unless it is forbidden by local law to do so. Some managers require the first glass of water to be poured into glasses at the water station or the bar. This is so ice can be easily placed in the glass before the water, in order to prevent spillage of ice and water at the table.

Whether to add a glass or not to this set up is the decision of each establishment.

Notes:

"Modern Casual" Setting

A growing trend of informal dining has lead to the creation of a new form of set up. For the purpose of this manual, we will refer to this type of set up as Modern Casual. This set up style consists of simply rolling a set of flatware into a napkin, which is held together either by the use of a paper band (Figure 3-2) or a fold-in that locks the napkin in place (Figure 3-3). The rollup is usually placed in the center of the place setting, and occasionally a glass is also preset.

Among its many advantages is the fact that this setting type drastically reduces the time it takes a server to set a table, or reset a table should there be an adjustment in the number of guests. Additionally, it frees the tabletop for the guests' use by allowing them to easily push aside the setting until they are served and need to use it. Finally, this style allows the wait staff to prepare a large number of set ups ahead of the shift and keep them ready for use near or in the dining room.

Although often found in establishments that do not use tablecloths but do experience a high table turnover, more semi-formal establishments are also adopting this setting style.

Figure 3-2: Modern Set Up with
Napkin wrap

Figure 3-3: Modern Set Up with
Napkin tuck

Notes:

"Banquet" Setting

The Banquet setting used for the set up of a meal in which almost all of the items to be served have been pre-selected by the host. This set up is commonly used for large groups or special functions.

For banquets that serve a large number of courses with a variety of food items, it simply may not be possible to pre-set the table top with everything that will be needed for the meal. A balance must be struck between the numbers of servers required to handle flatware placements during service (which increases the price for the event) versus over-crowding tables with utensils.

To understand the impact, a banquet hosting 150 guests with each guest being served a soup, an appetizer, a salad, main course and dessert accompanied by a glass of champagne, water, white and red wine, plus coffee would mean the service team would need to perform a minimum of 2,550 different functions. This number does not include any of the other types of service to be performed, such as serving bread or pouring multiple glasses of wine per guest.

Banquets need to be pre-set whenever possible to ensure best possible service and efficiency.

When setting up for a banquet, start the organization of flatware from the outside towards the inside. In most cases, Sauce spoons and Broth spoons that accompany a dish are not placed down during the set up unless really needed. Instead, the wait staff will generally put the appropriate spoon down with the specific course, just before serving the course.

To show the progression of a banquet meal, the example below demonstrates how and why each utensil is placed. *Here is the menu:*

Consommé of Spring Vegetables

Seared Scallops

Mesclun Salad

Poached Sea Bass

Dessert

Notes:

Consomme of
Spring Vegetables

***

Seared Scallops

***

Mesclun Salad

***

Poached Sea Bass

***

Dessert

Figure 3-4: Banquet Set Up

Figure 3-5: Banquet - First Course

<u>Set Up</u> is shown in Figure 3-4.
As the first course to be served is a
Consommé, the Bouillon spoon is
placed during the set up.

<u>First course</u> (Figure 3-5) is a *Consommé
which only needs the Bouillon spoon.*

Notes:

Figure 3-6: Banquet - Second Course

<u>Second course</u> (Figure 3-6)
Seared scallops, which is an Entremet, is to be served next. The spoon used in the first course was cleared with the consommé.

The Entremet fork and knife are ready for the second course. Even though this dish will likely include a sauce, a sauce spoon was eliminated from the set up so as not to confuse the guest or overcrowd the table.

Servers could place the sauce spoon down at this time, or upon request.

Figure 3-7: Banquet - Third Course

<u>Third course</u> (Figure 3-7)
The following course is a Mesclun Salad. Again, the use of an Entremet fork and knife is required. This picture shows that the set of silver used for the scallops was removed, and that another set of Entremet silverware remains for the salad service.

At this course, customers often get confused and use a mix of utensils. With this in mind, it is good practice to have more flatware available for adjustments.

Notes:

Figure 3-8: Banquet - Fourth Course

Fourth course (Figure 3-8)
Next the Poached Sea Bass is served. The main course is a fish dish and, therefore, justifies a Fish fork and knife. If the fish is served in a deep plate (like the ones used for Bouillabaisse) and with a broth, this dish would then also justify a Entremet spoon (to be used as a Broth spoon). Just like for the scallops, the broth spoon can be pre-set or added later.

Fifth course (Figure 3-9)
Dessert is served last. At this point, all other flatware should be removed from the table, leaving only the dessert and coffee flatware.

Since the dessert flatware is still located parallel to the guest, there are two ways to move it to its correct position. One option is to let the guest move his/her silverware to the pictured location himself. The more elegant option is for the server to walk clockwise around the table, moving the flatware down and in position for each guest.

One final note, the placement order would be from top to bottom. First move the spoon, then the fork, and finally, the knife (if there is one).

Figure 3-9: Banquet - Fifth Course

Notes:

Styles of Service

American Service (Individual Plate Service)

Europe, Canada and number of other countries as well as the American traditionalists refer to this technique of service as "*A l'assiette*" service, which translates to "service on the plate."

This is the most popular type of service in today's restaurants. This service style has been widely accepted because it is simple and quick, uses a minimum amount of serving equipment, and meets a wide variety of service needs. The food is plated in the kitchen and individually served to guests.

Figure 4-1: Service by the right
Preferred method

Figure 4-2: Service by the left
Tolerated method

The plate is presented from the guest's right (Figure 4-1) with the server's right hand. When asked to carry more than one plate, most individuals will pick them up with the right hand and load them on their left arm, even if they are left-handed.

If your instinct, however, is to pick plates up with your left hand and load them on your right arm (and it is too difficult to retrain to the other way) then you should serve by the left using the left hand, as is shown in Figure 4-2.

Notes:

| Figure 4-3: Improper service from the guest's right | Figure 4-4: Improper service from the guest's left |

The above servers demonstrate the consequences of a left-handed person serving from the right (Figure 4-3) and a right-handed person serving from the left (Figure 4-4).

Notice how the server invades the guest's space with his elbow, possibly making the guest uncomfortable or requiring him/her to move out of the way.

Notes:

Figure 4-5: Right way to deliver
multiple plates

Figure 4-6: Wrong way to deliver
multiple plates

The server in Figure 4-5 shows proper technique as he presents the first plate to the lady by the right, with his right hand. This is done while holding the gentleman's plate with his left hand, behind the lady's head.

Now notice the awkwardness of the server's position when he serves the first plate by the right with his left hand. In Figure 4-6, the lady must move aside not to be touched by the waiter's arm, and the gentleman must also move back because the other plate is too close to his face.

Notes:

Other Types of Service Styles

Although the service styles below aren't required for you to learn at the associate level, it's still a good idea to understand there are more ways to serve your guests.

Figure 4-7: **English Service**

Figure 4-8: **Russian Service**

English Service is a traditional method. The server presents the platter from the left side, and using service flatware, serves the guest directly on his/her plate

Russian Service is when the food is brought out of the kitchen on platters and serving dishes, and finished in front of the guest on a side table.

The plates are then placed in front of the guests just like American service. In the United States, diners often refer to this type of service as "French" service.

Notes:

Figure 4-9: French Service

Figure 4-10: Cloche Service

French Service is a traditional technique which is performed almost exclusively in French Embassies and at official French functions.

This method of service involves the server presenting a platter on the left side of each guest and having them help themselves.

Cloche Service is a traditional technique in which the food is either plated in the kitchen or in the dining room and then covered with a dome.

All plates are presented and unveiled at the same time.

Notes:

Clearing

Overview

Let's face it. There is nothing pretty about clearing a table of used dishes and flatware. Utilizing the correct clearing technique can, at least, help keep the server's fingers clean and maintain a smooth-looking service at the same time.

When clearing, it is desirable to be as discreet as possible. To this end, there are two main schools of thought regarding clearing a course:

1. *One theory considers that a maximum of two plates should be cleared at a time.* This avoids having to push the remaining food from one plate to another at the table where the guests could see it. Even though this theory is very discreet, it requires more trips for larger parties, or more servers, which can become as obtrusive to the guests as a single server arranging the plates in his/her arm behind the backs of the guests.

2. *The other theory considers that arranging the plates on the server's arm out of the view of guests is fine as long as it is well done and maintains discretion.*

Each restaurant must choose the clearing standards that best fit its dining room. For example, a restaurant may determine that it is acceptable to clear a Deuce (table of two persons) all at once, while requiring servers to make two trips for larger parties:

- One for the plates, and
- A second for all other items.

In general, it is desirable to clear clockwise around a table and to start clearing with a lady. This is especially true if the party consists of only a man and a woman) unless:

- A plate has a large amount of uneaten food, bones or other items. This plate should be cleared last, if possible, to avoid carrying all the leftovers around the table (for all to see) while clearing the rest of the table.
- If the table is set in such a way that it is not possible to walk full circle around it, start clearing from the dead-end (the location that has only one way out) in order to finish the clearing in an open area. This prevents a server from getting trapped in the dead-end with an arm loaded with dirty dishes.

Notes:

Clearing Guidelines

No matter what clearing procedure is selected for the dining room, the following guidelines apply:

- Effort must be made to be as discreet as possible.
- Generally, plates are only cleared from a table when all guests are finished, unless the guest pushes the plate away or asks it to be removed.
- Clearing is done by the right side of the guest, using the server's right hand.
- When clearing the main course, other items to be cleared at the same time include the bread & butter utensils and salt & pepper shakers.
- When finished eating a food item a guest should place his/her flatware (used and unused) parallel inside the plate, with the handles resting on the rim. If there is still food in the plate however, the server should wait a few minutes after the flatware is put down and check with the guest before clearing, as all guests do not follow this dining protocol.
- In formal dining, if a guest has moved his/her plate away, the plate should be removed and replaced with a Show plate.
- If a guest happens to be toying with an item the server desires to remove, it should be left on the table, without comment from the server. The server should return later to retrieve the item.
- If a guest appears to still be nibbling on bread, ask the guest if he/she would like to keep the bread. Do not try to take the bread.
- If a guest is blocking access to an item to be removed, the server should discreetly state the intent before physically attempting to clear the item.
- If the server is in the process of clearing and a guest begins to eat again, stop clearing immediately. Finish clearing when all are definitely done. If the other guests want to be cleared, in most cases they will make eye contact or ask the server directly.

Notes:

How to Clear

Using the proper technique to clear will help a server minimize the disruption to the table.

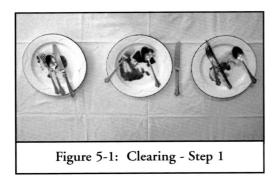

Figure 5-1: Clearing - Step 1

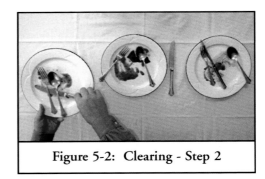

Figure 5-2: Clearing - Step 2

Figure 5-1 shows three plate settings. One of the settings has a piece of flatware remaining on the table and another has leftover food items in the plate. To start, pick up the first plate and lock it with your hand keeping the thumb and fourth finger above the edge of the rim. Lock the knife under the other flatware as shown in Figure 5-2.

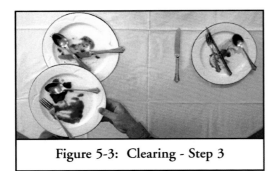

Figure 5-3: Clearing - Step 3

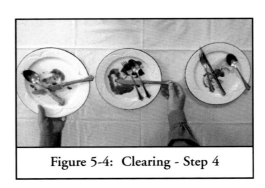

Figure 5-4: Clearing - Step 4

A piece of *flatware that is laying next to a plate should NOT be left on the table when picking up* the associated plate (Figure 5-3). Instead, pick up the flatware and place it on the plate, just like the server pictured in Figure 5-4. Then remove the plate from the table.

Notes:

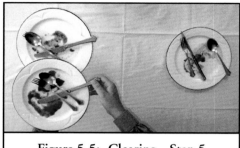

Figure 5-5: Clearing - Step 5

Figure 5-6: Clearing - Step 6

The second plate (with all the flatware on it) is then placed on the server's arm (Figure 5-5).

The second setting's flatware is taken from the second plate and placed on the first plate, aligning the fork and spoons with the ones from the first plate and locking the knife with the other one under the other flatware, as in Figure 5-6.

Figure 5-7: Clearing - Step 7

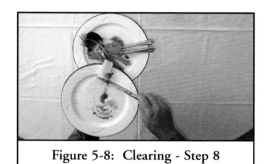

Figure 5-8: Clearing - Step 8

Pick up the third and final plate. This plate has some food in it, and it is placed on top of the second plate (Figure 5-7). Use the flatware of the third plate to slide the food onto the first plate where the flatware is lined up, shown in Figure 5-8.

Notes:

Figure 5-9: Clearing - Step 9

Figure 5-10: Clearing - Step 10

Migrate the third set of flatware to the first plate in the same manner as done for the second plate (Figure 5-9).   End the procedure by placing the first plate on the top of the third one, as in Figure 5-10.

The clean, easy to carry, and well-organized stack (Figure 5-11) can now be taken to the kitchen.

Figure 5-11: Clearing - Take away

Notes:

Clearing a Course

For all courses except the one directly before the dessert course, only the guests' plates are cleared.

The server picks up the lady's plate first (Figure 5-12) from her right side, and continues clockwise around the table.

Notice that the server never presents himself square to the table. Instead, the server's body position is always at an angle, to minimize the feel of his presence.

Next, the server moves in between the guests, and picks up the gentleman's plate (Figure 5-13) while holding the first plate behind him.

The server then steps away from the table. Notice that once the plates were picked up, they remained out of the guests' sight.

Figure 5-12: Clearing a course - Step 1

Figure 5-13: Clearing a course - Step 2

Notes:

Clearing the Entire Table

Start the clearing in the same order of precedence that was selected for prior course clearing. In this example, the lady's plate (Figure 5-14) is picked up first. The server moves behind her in order to arrange the flatware out of her sight (Figure 5-15.) The flatware is arranged according to the technique presented in the Proper Stacking Technique chapter in this section.

Figure 5-14: Clearing the table - Step 1

Figure 5-15: Clearing the table - Step 2

The server then moves in between the lady and the gentleman and picks up the man's plate, as in Figure 5-16. The server then steps aside to stack the plate on his arm and arranges the flatware out of the gentleman's sight (Figure 5-17).

Figure 5-16: Clearing the table - Step 3

Figure 5-17: Clearing the table - Step 4

Notes:

Stepping back in between the two guests, the server picks up the lady's B&B plate (shown in Figure 5-18), making sure that the B&B knife is stable on the plate and will not fall off. Again, the server steps aside to perform all the arranging of B&B plates, knives, etc. cleared from the table. The server always works BEHIND the guests' back as shown in Figure 5-17 and 5-18. Never work directly at the table, as pictured in Figure 5-19.

Figure 5-18: Clearing the table - Step 5

Figure 5-19: Wrong way to clear the table

The server carries a neat, well organized, easy to carry stack (Figure 5-20) back to the kitchen.

The server discreetly consolidated all cleared items as he progressed, and always worked behind the guest.

Note: If this table had contained four guests, it would have been preferable to simply clear the plates first and then return with a small tray to pick up the remaining items from the table.

Figure 5-20: Clearing stack

Notes:

3 | General Practices

This lesson shows how to:

- Properly handle menus.

- Perform bread and butter service.

- Perform mineral water & tap water service.

- Crumb a table.

- Take an order.

- Perform coffee service.

LESSON THREE

General Practices

Objectives

By the end of this lesson, you should be able to...

- Handle a menu properly.

- List, describe and demonstrate the most common methods of bread and butter service, according to the standards demonstrated by the mentor.

- Perform mineral and tap water service according to the standard demonstrated by the mentor.

- Correctly record an order, showing the differences between a woman and man.

- Explain the difference between a regular coffee, an espresso and a cappuccino.

- Perform two methods of crumbing.

General Practices

Menu Presentation

Menu presentation varies depending on the restaurant. For many restaurants, the menu is a tool to inform guests of what is available for their dining enjoyment. For others, it is a fashion statement. Some servers take menu presentation as an opportunity to show style, elegance or to set the tone for the meal.

Restaurants can have menus for:

- Aperitifs
- Ordering of the meal
- Prix fixe menu meals
- Desserts
- After dinner drinks, port or dessert wines

And of course there is the famous wine list, which sometimes is divided into at least two menus: the main wine list and the "reserve" wine list.

Once the restaurant determines the right balance of menus, *it is critical that menus are clean before they are presented to guests.* Some restaurants have separate lunch and dinner menus. If so, **they wipe them with linen soaked with sanitizer between shifts.**

The actual presentation of the menu to the guests can set the tone and speed for the meal. In an establishment where guests are not expected to spend the entire evening, the menus are usually given right at the seating.

If the restaurateur desires to hurry the party, the server may present the menus open to the guest to block their view and focus them on making a selection (Figure 6-1). Most will offer the menu and take the drink orders, which allows guests a time to relax and focus on their dining enjoyment. If the restaurant wants to set a relaxed tone to encourage guests to stay a bit longer, the server can wait until the guests are seated, and have given their drink orders before offering the menus. One way to use menus is like this:

1. Seat the guests,
2. Present them with an Aperitif menu,
3. Take a drink order, and
4. Bring the drinks.

Notes:

Later on, when the server thinks the guests are ready, he or she will ask the host (or the party if no one identified him/herself as the host) for permission to bring the meal's menus.

As you can see, methods vary with each establishment. The main thing to remember is that there are many ways to use the menu to speed or slow service. The menu can be viewed either as an accelerator or as a brake in order to speed up or slow down the time guests spend at the table.

Figure 6-1: Presentation of the menu

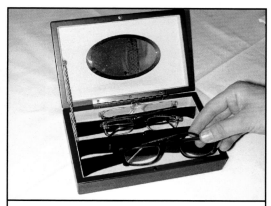

Figure 6-2: Reading glasses for customers

Some establishments carry two different sets of menus for each service:

1. *One set with pre-printed prices, as is commonplace; and*
2. *A set of menus without prices shown on them.*

This second set of menus is to be provided to hosted guests and women (when they are not the host). There is no reason for a person that is being invited to know about the price of what is being offered.

The menu must be uncomplicated and comfortable for the guest to read or the establishment should make available a few pairs of reading glasses for guest use, as in Figure 6-2. Glasses should be wiped with a sanitizing solution between each use.

Notes:

Proper menu handling guidelines include the following points:

- Each menu should be checked to ensure that the insert(s), if applicable, are in place and it is clean prior to being handed to a guest.
- Always count the number of menus in your hand before approaching the table, to make sure that there is one for each customer.
- Do not interrupt a conversation to present menus.
- Menus should be presented in the same order of precedence as the one used for service: ladies first, unless there is a guest of honor at the table or another specific protocol.
- The menu is presented by circling the table, handing a menu to each guest by their right side; _not_ distributed by reaching across the table from a single location (Figure 6-3).
- Dessert menus should only be presented when the table is ready for dessert (completely cleared and crumbed), as shown in Figure 6-4.
- If guests have utensils or drinks dangerously close to the menu, the server should warn them or assist in moving the item out of the way.
- If a guest fails to respond to the menu presentation because he/she is involved in a conversation and does not wish to relinquish attention from the table's activity, the server should pass up the guest and come back later, rather than trying to force the menu down or try to place it in the plate.

Figure 6-3: Don't hand across the table

Figure 6-4: Dessert menu presentation

Notes:

Bread Service

Serving bread and butter is almost automatic in virtually every establishment. However, *when* the bread is served varies considerably from one restaurant to another, depending on style and motive. Bread and butter is commonly served:

- Immediately after the guests are seated and have received water. This could be a welcoming gesture, such as a specialty bread.
- Following a complimentary small hors d'oeuvre, also referred to as an *Amuse Bouche*.
- After the food order has been taken.

The following are some of the more common ways restaurants serve bread to guests.

Classic Bread Service

This classic technique is seen in Figure 6-5, and is widely used. *The server places the bread in the center of the table.*

The basket is sometimes lined with a cloth.

Figure 6-5: Classic Bread Service

Figure 6-6: English Bread Service

English Bread Service

This method is shown in Figure 6-6, and goes along with the English Service style.

The server carries the bread in a basket and puts a piece in each guest's B&B plate.

Notes:

Assorted Bread Service

This service is a variation of the English Bread Service. A basket (Figure 6-7) is filled with a few different kinds of breads and presented to the guest. There are two common variations for the guest to retrieve the bread:

1. The server serves the guests, or
2. The guest helps themselves from the basket directly.

Figure 6-7: Assorted Bread Service

Banquet Bread Service

Figure 6-8 shows the way bread is often preset for banquets or special functions. The bread is simply placed on the B&B plate prior to the arrival of guests. This technique frees the staff from having to handle the bread in the first few minutes of the seating, allowing them to focus on guests needs during that time. This technique is very effective for very large parties.

Figure 6-8: Banquet Bread Service

Notes:

Butter Service

Butter is presented to guests in a variety of shapes and sizes--from prepackaged squares to a restaurant's special recipe and design.

Butter is divided into three main categories:

1. Salted butters.
2. Unsalted butters.
3. Specialty, such as flavored or battered butters.

Butter may be served in creative shapes in addition to a flavor. Typically, a butter's flavoring relates to the style of cuisine, i.e. *Garlic Butter* in Italian and Mediterranean restaurants.

Figure 6-9: Butter in a cup

The way butter is served to a table is usually based on the type of equipment available in the establishment. Dining rooms that have an elaborate inventory of silver may serve butter in a special buttercup (Figures 6-9 and 6-10).

Butter cups are generally made out of silver and divided in two compartments. The stem, or bottom portion, is shaped like a cup and can accommodate ice or be empty. The top portion, a saucer, contains the butter and sometimes ice. The saucer is equipped with holes that let the cold air flow through and keep the butter cool (if ice is in the stem) or allow water from the dripping ice to separate from the butter. The buttercup is placed in the center of the table for all guests to access.

Figure 6-10: Buttercup service

Notes:

Another common way to server butter is to place it in a B&B plate (typically located either at the center of the table or between every two guests), as seen in Figure 6-11.

If guests use a lot of butter, more plates can be spread around the table. Do not overfill the B&B plates.

Figure 6-11: Butter on a B&B plate

A slightly more casual way to serve butter is to place butter that is prepackaged into individually-wrapped packets.

Servers simply put the butter on a B&B plate (generally counting one or two per person) and place it on the table, as in Figure 6-12.

Figure 6-12: Individually-wrapped butter

Notes:

Water Service

In the United States, it is traditional to serve water to guests at their arrival unless it is against the law.

Serving water in the United States requires the server's attention throughout the meal.

There are two distinct kinds of water service:

1. *Mineral water or bottled water, and*
2. *Tap water.*

Both service types are performed by the right side of the guest, holding the bottle or pitcher with the right hand.

Notes:

Mineral and Bottled Water

People usually drink mineral or bottled water to enjoy the:

1. Taste.
2. Bubbles in sparkling water.

What you need to know:

1. *Mineral water is served without ice.*
2. *The glass used for serving mineral water is usually a different shape than the regular water glass.*
3. *Fill up the glass using a smooth, elegant pour.* Hold the bottle by its bottom half, with the label facing the guest as shown in Figure 6-13.
4. *Serve by the right with the right hand.*

Figure 6-14 demonstrates incorrect pouring technique.

Figure 6-13: Do pour water like this

Figure 6-14: Don't pour this way

Notes:

Tap water service

As serving water is a task you will perform several times throughout your guests' meal, you need to know that Tap water can be served three ways:

1. *At the bar or waiter station.*
   - Glasses are pre-filled with ice;
   - Water is added later;
   - Filling glasses is quick, easy and offers the opportunity to wipe off overspills from glasses, if necessary.

   Another advantage of this technique is that it provides the server the opportunity to offer guests a choice between mineral and tap water.

2. *Directly in the glasses that are on the table.* This means that the water will be poured in front of the guest (Figure 6-15).

3. *By picking up the glass from the table and pouring by the side of the table, as in Figure 6-16.*

Figure 6-15: Pouring water with the glass on the table

Figure 6-16: Picking up the glass to pour water

You may be required to pour ice and water into a glass from a pitcher that restricts the flow of ice from its spout. In such situation the *preferred* method is that you fill the glass at the waiter station. Pouring directly at the table from the side of the pitcher in order to allow ice/water to flow into the glass, however, is ONLY done as a last option.

Notes:

Order Taking

There are a number of industry-standard codes utilized to record specific information about a guest. These codes help communicate who and what is ordered and are used by the kitchen staff as well as the servers.

One type of code describes the seat position of each guest. Position numbers are used as locators, associating ordered items to a specific guest. Many dining rooms have a numbering system that assigns numbers to each table and their seats. In many cases, the seat numbered "1" will be in a consistent place, such as the seat positioned with the back toward the Maitre D' desk. Proceeding clockwise around the table, all remaining seats locations are numbered sequentially.

Another code is often used to tell if the guest is man or woman. The woman identifier is a circle around the seat number. *Why?* This identifier helps the restaurant serve ladies first.

And finally, underlining a seat number signals that a change to the recipe is requested. The type of modification is described next to the underlined position number.

<u>Order taking example:</u> A party of three is seated at Table 3. The gentleman is in Position 1, the lady is in Position 2, and a second gentleman is in Position 3. The party orders drinks prior to their meal. The first gentleman orders a beer, the lady orders a Seabreeze cocktail, and the second gentleman orders a Martini. Figure 6-17 shows how to correctly record the above order. The total number of items ordered is written on the left-hand side of the pad. The guest information is put on the right-hand side of the ordered item.

Figure 6-17: Taking an order

Reading from the pad, the order is:
> *One Beer for Position 1,*
> *One Seabreeze for Position 2 (woman)*
> *One Martini for Position 3.*

Buzzwords and Common Abbreviations

To record food items on an order most establishments have established a list of buzzwords. A buzzword is an abbreviation of the dish name. Buzzwords are shorthand for servers. Good buzzwords are kept as short as possible, but are long enough to differentiate each dish. For

Notes:

example, a dish named Black Angus Sirloin Steak Melanie on the menu would probably have a buzzword such as "Sirloin." If the menu featured more than one sirloin selection, however, then the buzzword would probably be "Sirloin Melanie." Another acceptable variation could be "Melanie," as long as there are not other dishes containing the word "Melanie."

The most common dining room abbreviations are listed beside:

From the Most cooked to the least cooked

Well Done: **W**
Medium Well: **MW**
Medium: **M**
Medium Rare : **MR**
Rare: **R**
Extra Rare: **X Rare**
Blackened or Black & Blue: **BLKN**

Other Basic abbreviations
Sauce on the Side: **SOS**
Light on the Sauce: **LOS**
Out of Stock: **86**

Note that generally, and unless specified otherwise by the guests, when an order is uneven (some guests do not have appetizers while others do) it is preferable to serve the few appetizers by themselves, and then serve all the main courses together so guests finish together.

Crumbing

Crumbing a table is the removal of breadcrumbs from a tabletop.

Wipe the table of crumbs prior to serving dessert, whether it's an individual table or a banquet table.

Sometimes the tablecloth may be messy from bread or other foods during prior courses. Crumbing should also be performed in those cases.

Figure 6-18: Crumbing into a plate

The traditional technique consists of wiping the crumbs off the tablecloth with a folded napkin (Figure 6-18) into a B&B plate.

Notes:

Using a Crumber

The majority of establishments (and dining room professionals) now use a special device called a Crumber. This long, curved blade is generally made from a lightweight metal, and is designed to scoop crumbs off the tabletop.

Crumbers are very economical and are about the size of a pen. They fit perfectly in a server's pocket along with whatever item the server uses to write.

Note: If there is sauce on the tablecloth, use a napkin since crumbers act like a windshield wiper and spread the sauce across the tablecloth.

Figure 6-19: Gather the crumbs

Figure 6-20: Crumbs in a napkin

Steps to crumb:
1. Place the edge of the crumber on the tablecloth.
2. Gather the crumbs by gently scooping them into the curved portion of the crumber (Figure 6-19).
3. Lift it off the table.
4. Dump the crumbs onto a B&B plate (or napkin).

Note: In very upscale dining, crumbs are first dumped on top of the folded napkin. Then the server holds the crumber under the plate while the crumbs on the napkin are dumped into the B&B plate, as in Figure 6-20. The napkin is then used as a cover to conceal the crumbs from the guests.

Notes:

Coffee Service

Coffee and specialty coffees have become very popular in both formal and casual dining.

There are as many ways to serve coffee as there are types of coffee. For now though, let's just learn ways to serve the traditional type of coffee - regular or decaffeinated.

Regular / Decaf Coffee

Correct coffee service starts with good tray organization. The bar tray in Figure 6-21 contains:

1. A pot of regular / decaf coffee.

2. A creamer.

3. Sugar and a selection of artificial sweeteners.

4. Coffee saucer, cup and spoon.

Figure 6-21: Coffee tray

Even though the following example shows a coffee service performed in one sequence, the service could also be performed in two steps.

The server would first deliver all the coffee items *except* the pot of coffee.

The server would then make a second trip to deliver the coffee pot.

Notes:

Figure 6-22: Creamer / Sugar Service

Figure 6-23: Coffee pour at table

The server presents himself by the right side of the guest (as in Figure 6-22). The sugar set up is placed on the table first, with the creamer next. The coffee cup plus its saucer and spoon is last.

Pour the coffee slowly holding the spout of the coffee pot close to the cup's rim (Figure 6-23) so that a guest has time to let the server know when to stop. This avoids splashing the coffee over the rim.

Figure 6-24: Coffee pour on tray

Figure 6-25: Coffee cup delivery

Here's another way to serve coffee.
Instead of filling the cup as it rests on the table, the server fills the cup with coffee on the tray (Figure 6-24) and then places the cup on the table, as in Figure 6-25.

Notes:

This type of coffee service is fast and efficient and is a popular method for serving larger parties or serving parties that don't want interruptions.

Note: Providing coffee service for an entire table requires the cream and sugar set be placed in the center of the table, where each guest has access to it. A table of six or more guests usually requires two sets, placed on opposite ends of the table.

Traditionally, there are two ways to place the spoon on the saucer as shown in the two figures below.

Figure 6-26: Spoon is on top

Figure 6-27: Spoon is on the side

Figure 6-26 shows placing the spoon horizontally with the spoon's handle on the right. A horizontal spoon placement gives the guest easy access to the handle of the spoon for mixing in sugar or cream.

Figure 6-27 shows vertical spoon placement, which is used when individually wrapped sugar cube(s) are under the cup's handle, locking the spoon in place and eliminating noise while being carried across the dining room. This set up is commonly referred to as "Room Service".

The least desirable placement is to put the handles of both the cup and spoon at the 4 or 5 o'clock position. This makes it more difficult to pick up either the cup or the spoon without moving both out of place.

Notes:

Espresso

An Espresso is a coffee that is made by pushing hot water at high pressure through a patty of finely ground coffee beans, seen in Figure 6-28. The end result looks like the cups in Figure 6-29.

Figure 6-28: Making Espresso

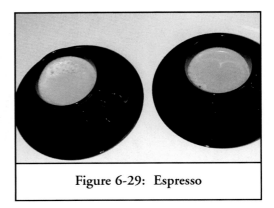

Figure 6-29: Espresso

Cappuccino

The popularity of this type of drink has sky-rocketed in the United States in recent years, creating a number of variations on the original recipe.

Figure 6-30 is an example of a cup of Cappuccino. The drink is a combination of espresso and steamed milk froth.

The original recipe calls for a "milk froth" made from steamed milk to rest on top of espresso coffee. From there, the amount of milk, or no milk at all is a matter of personal preference, even though traditionalists insist that there should be no milk, only "froth."

Figure 6-30: Cappuccino

Notes:

Notes:

4 | Beer & Cocktails

This lesson contains information on:

- Beer Essentials.

- Beer Service.

- Cocktail Essentials.

LESSON FOUR

Beer & Cocktails

Objectives

By the end of this lesson, you should be able to...

- List and explain four (4) ingredients to make beer.

- List nine steps (9) to make beer, with 80% accuracy.

- Explain the difference between the two categories of beer.

- Perform beer service in a pilsner glass.

- List the four components of a cocktail order.

- List and explain the most common cocktail mixing methods.

Beer and Cocktails

Beer Essentials

Beer is recorded as one of the oldest beverages humans have produced, dating back as far back as the 5th millennium BC in records of Ancient Egypt and Mesopotamia! Today, beer is still enjoyed by countless billions in nearly every language around the world.

Beer Ingredients

Generally speaking, beer is a bitter-tasting alcoholic drink brewed by fermenting malt and yeast, and then flavoring it with hops. **Beer is made from four very basic ingredients:**

1. Water.
2. Fermentable Sugar (Malted Barley).
3. Hops.
4. Yeast.

Water

Water used to make beer need only to be drinkable and low in chlorine levels. This is the largest ingredient, by volume, of all the ingredients. Some commercial breweries chemically treat the water used in the brewing process to make sure this key ingredient is the same for every brewing, with a desired "hardness" and pH.

Fermentable Sugar (Malted Barley)

The fermentable sugar used to make beer is made from malted barley. Barley is a cereal plant with a long head of whiskered grains (Figure 7-1) that has many uses, one of which happens to be the production of malt. Rice, corn, and pure sugar are sometimes used as a less expensive substitute, but those options add little to the overall flavor. Malt is the backbone of beer because it creates a strong, sweet flavor.

It is malt that determines the beer's overall body (the way the beer feels in your mouth) and final color / flavor.

Figure 7-1: Barley

Notes:

Hops

Hops come from a climbing vine of the mulberry family. Its green, female flowers look like little pinecones. It is these flowers that are then dried and used in the brewing process to add a distinctive bitter taste to the beer.

Hops also act as a preservative by lowering the amount of bacteria that can grow in beer.

Hops are what give the beer its "head", or foam, at the top of the glass.

Figure 7-2: Hops

Yeast

Yeast is a single-celled living organism that lives its whole life cycle during the beer making process. *Yeast feeds off of the sugars in the malt.* As it feeds, the yeast creates alcohol and carbon dioxide, and gives the beer its flavor and carbonation.

Yeast is the final factor of the style and flavor of the beer. Although there are many hundreds of different types of yeast, they can be divided into two separate categories:

1. Ale yeast.
2. Lager yeast.

The Brewmaster determines what type of yeast to use depending on the style of beer that is being brewed.

Without yeast, the mix of ingredients would not ferment, and beer would not be created!

Notes:

Brewing Beer

The process of brewing beer is an age-old technique changing very little over the course of time.

Beer making is done in the following steps:

1. Malted grain is passed through a milling machine that cracks the dried kernals and grinds them into a course powder.

2. Cracked malt from Step 1 is then mixed with hot water. This makes a thick, sweet liquid called "wort". —*alla ws)h*

3. Bring the wort to a boil.

4. Boil, or brew, the wort for up to two hours adding hops a little at a time.

5. Cool the mixture and add desired amount of yeast.

6. Move the cooled wort to a holding tank, where the yeasts slowly converts the sugar to alcohol.

7. Move the mixture to a second tank, where sugar is added, which re-energizes the yeast. The yeast consumes the sugar and creates bubbles (carbon dioxide - CO_2).

8. Bottle the beer, trapping the CO_2.

9. Put the bottles through a heating process, called pasteurization.

Pasteurization is sometimes done to kill any remaining yeast or other microorganisms.

Types of Beer

Beers can be broken down into two major categories:

1. Ales.
2. Lagers.

The difference between these two groups is in how they are brewed and the type of yeast used in the brewing process. There are literally thousands of different strains of yeast available to the brewer and each will give off its own unique flavor to the finished product.

Ales and lagers can be further broken down into many sub-categories and styles.

Notes:

Ales

Generally, ales are rich in character and dark in color.

Ales use top-fermenting yeasts at warmer temperatures between 55 and 75 degrees Fahrenheit. *The time to produce ale beer is usually short.* The major categories of ales include Stouts, Wheat beer, Trappist/Abbey ales, Brown ales, Pale ales, Saison and Porters.

Stouts

Stouts are generally made from pale or caramel malts and roasted un-malted barley. Typical stouts are known for their very dark black color, creamy white head, and rich flavor. Generally, stouts tend to have a heavy barley character and a low hop rate. Beers in this category span a taste range from sweetness to bitterness.
Examples: Guinness®, Irish "Dry" Stouts

Wheat beer

Wheat beers use a high proportion of malted wheat to create a fuller bodied, highly effervescent, low-alcohol beer. They generally have a cloudy, bright yellow appearance and smell of vanilla, clove and often banana.
Examples: Hefeweizen ('hefe' is German for yeast) and Weissbire, or "white beer"

Trappist / Abbey ales

In order to be truly labeled Trappist, these beers must be brewed in one of six Belguim brewing monasteries; otherwise they are referred to as Abbey Ales. *This style of ale is commonly dark amber in color, full-bodied, moderate to high in alcohol, and have a special bottle, which results in yeasty sediments.*

Brown ales

Brown ales are generally brown in color, slightly sweet and have lightly hopped features. Some brown ales, such as the Newcastle Brown, are somewhat nutty in taste. This character is because roasted caramel malt is used during brewing.
Examples: Winter, Scottish, Irish, and cream ales

Notes:

Pale ales

Pale ales are typically amber or copper in color, drawing from the use of pale malts and tend to be slightly dry and bitter.
Example: India Pale Ale or I.P.A.

Saison

Saison beers tend to be light in color and body. They are brewed slightly higher in alcohol, and have a typical fruity sourness.

Porter

Generally medium-bodied and dark in color, porters vary in alcohol content, bitterness, and hop rate, but lack the bite of roasted barley found in their cousin, the stout.

British Ales
  Bitter
  Mild
  Pale Ale
  Brown Ale
  Stout
  Barley Wine
  Porter
  Scottish Ale
Wheat Beers
  Weizenbier
  Unkelweizen
  Belgian Lambic
  American Wheat Beer

German Ale
  Altbier
  Kölsh
American Cream Ale
Belgian Specialty Ale
  Saison
  White Beer
  Trappist Ale

Figure 7-3: Ale Beer Examples

Notes:

Lagers

Typical lagers are light in body and color, and have a crisp taste.

Lagers use bottom-fermenting yeasts at cooler temperatures between 32 and 55 degrees Fahrenheit. *The process to produce lager beer can be long. Because of the cooler temperature that lagers ferment, they are less likely to grow bacteria during the fermentation step.*

The major categories of ales include Pilsner, German bock / Dopplebock, Oktoberfest, Vienna-style lagers, American / Australian lagers, and California Common / Steam Beer.

Pilsner

Pilsners are generally pale golden in color, and light and crisp to the taste. Czech pilsners present a richly sweet malt-laden brew with a lots of bubbles. German pilsners, 'Pils' for short, tend to be more bitter than the Czech types. *Pilsners often have spicy, floral flavors and smells. They also have a thick, rich head of foam.*

German bock / Dopplebock

These beers can be brewed either dark or light (helles) in color and range between 6 and 14 percent alcohol. German bocks are brewed to bring out the sweetness of the malt. Very little hops are used in this style. The goal is to use just enough to complement the rich malt flavor.

Oktoberfest

Oktoberfest beers are amber-orange in color. These highly malty brews are balanced by a noticable hop bitterness. Like it's counterpart Märzen (German for March), Oktoberfest beers are traditionally brewed in October in preparation for the fall festival.

Vienna-style

This beer type is similar to the beers of Oktoberfest with a red-amber to copper color, but have a much milder malt characteristic.
Example: Negra Modelo

Notes:

American / Australian lagers

By adding corn and rice to the brewing, these lagers are lighter than their closest relative, the Pilsner. American lager, also know as the American Standard variety of beer, is usually brewed with a mild hop amount. *This type of beer is the most popular in North America.*
<u>Example:</u> Budweiser, Coors, Molson, Fosters

California Common / Steam Beer

This type of beer is brewed at ale fermenting temperatures while using a special type of lager yeast. Brewed nearly exclusively by the Anchor Brewing Company in San Francisco, California, this beer typically has a malty sweetness because it uses caramel or crystal malt.

*German &
 Continental Lagers*
Pilsner
Oktoberfest
Märzen
Vienna Lager
Bock/Doppelbock
Munich Helles
Dunkel
Australian Lagers

American Lagers
American Standard
American Premium
Dry Beer
*California Common
 Beer*
American Dark Beers

Figure 7-4: Lager Beer Examples

Notes:

Beer Service

For nearly every type of beer brewed there is a glass that is considered appropriate for its service. In Belgium, it is actually common to have a beer that has been designed around the shape of the glass!

Just as the shape of a wine glass can be matched with different wines, so can the glass a beer is served in. <u>*Why?*</u>

Because the shape of the beer glass can impact the way a beer is enjoyed. The way a glass is shaped, along with the way the beer is poured into it, can change the amount of foam, or "head", that is created on top of the beer and also allows more of the unique flavors to be released.

Glassware for Beer

Generally speaking, the two most popular types of glasses are:

1. Pilsner.
2. Pint.

Pilsner Glass

This 12-ounce glass is used with a variety of light beer styles.

Originally designed to show off German lager beers, this tall, slender glass (Figure 7-5) has a wide mouth that tapers downward to a small pedestal or short-stemmed bottom.

The shape of this glass helps release the bubbles in the beer.

Figure 7-5: Pilsner Glass

Notes:

Pint Glass

This Tumbler style of glass is probably the most common glass used to serve beer in the United States.

Even though there are variations, the pint glass usually comes in two distinct sizes:

1. 16-ounce US Tumbler.
2. 20-ounce Imperial or Nonic.

The shape of this glass is generally round, but the 20-ounce style has a bump near the top that makes it easy to hold and easy to stack.

Figure 7-6: Pint Glass

Remember that when handling glassware, the rules of sanitation come first!

Besides keeping your hands and beer glasses clean, know that left-over soap from washing can also change the taste and presentation of beer. Usually, it is best to hand-wash beer glasses. If a film is still on the glasses after washing, they may need to be polished.

Even though it is fairly common to serve a cold glass with beer, if there is too much condensation on the inside of the glass, the beer's flavor might be diluted.

Be sure to know how your customer wants to enjoy his beer and offer him a choice of glassware!

Notes:

Pouring Beer

With so many different types and styles of beer -- and as just as many different glasses to pour them in -- there are a few different ways to get the beer from the bottle into the glass.

A number of customers like to pour their beer themselves. So when thinking about whether or not to pour the beer for a guest, it is best to ask them before you start!

To pour a beer into a Pilsner glass, follow this simple two-step process:

1. ***Bring a glass***, usually chilled, and the beer to the table.
2. ***Pour the beer*** gently against the inside of the glass. <u>*Two ways to do this are:*</u>

   a. Grab the rim of the glass with the lip of the bottle. Lean the glass over slightly tipping it gently (holding it stable with the lip of the bottle) and tilt the beer bottle's bottom up slowly so that beer flows smoothly against the inside of the glass (Figure 7-7). This option requires you pay close attention to how much the glass is tipped over. *No customer wants to get wet!*

   b. Don't touch the glass with the bottle, but pour the beer gently on the inside of the glass (Figure 7-8). This is easier to do if you pick up the glass and tilt it slightly, but it can be done by leaving the glass on the table.

Figure 7-7: Place the bottle on the rim

Figure 7-8: Pour beer against the side

For a Pint glass, simly pour the last bit of the beer directly in the center of the glass.

The result is a perfect amount of foam (aim for about 1/4 inch) that floats on top of the beer!

Notes:

Cocktail Essentials

The art of making cocktails is called "mixology".

There are many books published about mixology and there are literally thousands of cocktails. Even though each bar could make slight changes to a cocktail, the basic principles of mixology remain fairly standard.

The Four Components of a Cocktail Order

The making of almost every type of cocktail includes at least three out of the four following components:

1. *Alcohol.*
2. *Method.*
3. *Serving (Mixing and Style).*
4. *Garnish.*

Remember these four components and you can make sure you can explain to a bartender what the guest wants, even if you don't know how the cocktail is made!

Alcohol

Gather the following two pieces of information for the alcohol portion of the order:

1. <u>What category of alcohol should be used?</u>
   Many cocktails were created by using a specific kind of liquor. For example, the Martini originally was created with a base of Gin. Over time, many people replaced Vodka for Gin. *To be safe, check what type of alcohol a guest wants in the drink.*

2. <u>What brand of alcohol should be used?</u>
   Different brands (for the same type of liquor) really do taste different! But besides that, many people order a specific brand name as a status statement. Usually, when a guest wants a specific brand of alcohol, they normally mention it first. For example, a guest ordering a "Manhattan" (which main liquor is supposed to be whiskey) may ask for a "CC Manhattan". That signals that the drink is to be made with Canadian Club® whiskey.

Notes:

All alcohol brands are divided into four categories, each generally matched to a price range. These categories are generally named:

> *1. House Brands.*
> *2. Call Brands.*
> *3. Premium Brands.*
> *4. Top Shelf (Super Premium Brands).*

Which brands are put into each category can change from one restaurant to the next.

So it is important to know the way each establishment categorizes its liquors. Understanding these categories and the difference prices can benefit the guest, the server and the restuarant.

Method

Method means two things:

> *1. The way a cocktail is mixed, and*
> *2. What is its texture.*

The cocktail method is to a bartender what a cooking recipe is for a chef. The method is made up of ingredients *plus* the way the ingredients are mixed together. *Here are a couple examples of very well known methods:*

1. A Martini is 11/2 ounces of Gin and 1/2 ounces of dry Vermouth stirred with ice, but it can be asked for in the following ways:
   a. Extra Dry: 13/4 ounces of Gin and 1/4 ounce of dry Vermouth.
   b. Dry: 12/3 ounces of Gin and 1/3 ounce of dry Vermouth.
   c. Sweet: 11/2 ounce of Gin, 3/4 ounce of sweet Vermouth.
   d. Dirty: Add some of the olive juice to the mix.

2. Making a drink "Sour", which is adding the juice of half a lemon and half a teaspoon of powdered sugar. Today, Sour mixes are often pre-made for the bartender.
   Examples of liquor used with Sour are: Whiskey Sour, Gin Sour and Vodka Sour.

Notes:

Serving: Mixing & Style

There technically two pieces to the 'Serving' part of a coctail order: Mixing and Style.

Mixing

A cocktail order can include, even though it is rare, the description of the mixing method. Who will ever forget the famous line by the English spy, *007*, "Shaken, not stirred."

The most common mixing styles are:

       1) Shaken,   *2) Bruised, and*   *3) Stirred.*

Shaken

Shaken utilizes a shaker (Figure 7-9) that is partially filled with rock ice (Figure 7-10) plus the cocktail's ingredients. Utilizing a shaker (Figure 7-11) not only cools the mix, but also melts some of the ice into the mix, which slightly lightens the taste of the drink.

Figure 7-9: A Shaker

Figure 7-10: Adding ice

Figure 7-11: Shaking

Bruised

Signifies that the ingredients are placed in a shaker and shaken harder and longer than normal. The result is that some of the ice is reduced to small flakes that resemble 'bruises,' named because they appear clear, but are still solid.

Notes:

Stirred

When a drink is order 'Stirred', the bartender is being instructed by the customer to not shake the cocktail.

This means that the bartender must use a type of mixing spoon to gently stir the cocktail.

A type of spoon is shown in Figure 7-12.

The result is that the cocktail still gets chilled, just not as violently as when it is shaken, which means that less of the ice melts into the drink.

Customers who don't want to dilute their drink sometimes order their cocktail 'stirred'.

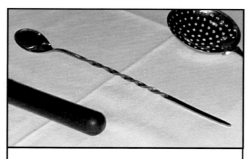

Figure 7-12: Stirring Spoon Example

Style

Most cocktails use ice as a step in their preparation. *Whether or not the ice is kept in with the mix depends on the style of serving.* **The style that a cocktail is served dictates the way the cocktail is presented to the guest. The style impacts:**

- *The type of glass used.*
- *The amount of ice in the mix.*
- *The texture.*

There are typically five main cocktail service styles:

1. On the Rocks.
2. Tall.
3. Up.
4. Neat.
5. Frozen.

Notes:

On The Rocks

The style means that a cocktail is served in some type of Rock glass filled with ice.

There are several ways a cocktail can be prepared "on the rocks." The easiest way is to put the ice into a glass and pour the alcohol on top, as shown below.

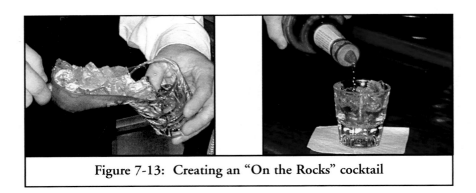

Figure 7-13: Creating an "On the Rocks" cocktail

Another alternative is to use the shaken method and then pour all the ingredients, including the ice, into a Rock glass.

A bartender may choose to strain the ice out from within the shaker so that the drink can be poured over fresh ice, as shown in Figure 7-14.

Figure 7-14: Alternative way to create an "On the Rocks" cocktail

Notes:

Tall

Tall is a serving that generally applies to mixtures that include a soft drink (such as club soda, Sprite®, Coke®, or even milk) and are served over ice.

A tall glass allows the bartender to vary the amount of the non-alcoholic mix to be added. That way, the bartender can change how strong a drink he makes.

Figure 7-15: Creating a "Tall" cocktail

Here is how to make a tall drink:
1. *Fill a glass with ice.*
2. *Pour the alcohol(s) into the glass.*
3. *Pour the non-alcoholic item into the glass, filling it up to the top.*

Another option is to then take the ingredients in the glass and either shake or stir them.

If soda is to be included, it is added last, topping off the glass.

Notes:

Up

A drink that is served "Up" is chilled with ice, but then served without it.

The cocktail ingredients are typically placed in a shaker (Figure 7-16) during preparation, but are sometimes stirred at the guest's request.

The drink is strained directly into a glass, which ideally is cold.

One example of a cocktail that is usually served this way is the Martini.

Martini glasses can either be maintained cold (by being stored in a refrigerator) or chilled at the time of service by being filled with ice water, which is thrown out before pouring the drink into the glass.

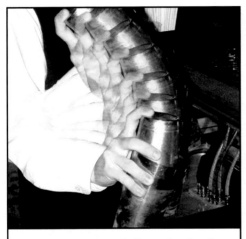

Figure 7-16: Chilling the drink

Figure 7-17: Serving "Up"

Notes:

Neat

A drink requested "Neat" signals to the bartender that the cocktail is served plain. That means it is not chilled with ice or had any other ingredient added.

The alcohol is simply poured into the glass and served to the customer.

A Neat serving can be presented in different kinds of glasses.

The restaurant usually chooses the type of glass that should be used.

Some examples are below (from left to right): a Rock glass, a Taster or Sherry glass, and a Snifter.

Figure 7-18: Glass options for serving a cocktail "Neat"

Notes:

Frozen

A cocktail served "Frozen" means that the alcohol(s) is blended with ice.

Drink has a slushy texture and often contains fruit flavors, like the example in Figure 7-19.

Figure 7-19: A "Frozen" drink

Figure 7-20: Add ingredients to the blender

Figure 7-21: Blend until smooth

The steps to make a frozen drink are:

1. All ingredients for the cocktail, including ice, are placed into a mixer (Figure 7-20).
2. Blend until the texture is smooth and free of ice chunks, in Figure 7-21.

Notes:

Garnish

A number of cocktails add a garnish, which complements the taste of the drink. Some places have the server add the garnish the drinks, while the bartender does it in other locations.

To hold garnishes, many places use a compartmentalized box (Figure 7-22) that is often called a fruit-bar or condiment-dispenser. It is often placed on the service bar.

The most common garnishes for cocktails are:

- *Olives*
- *Onion*
- *Lime Twist*
- *Lemon Twist*
- *Lime or Lemon Wedge*
- *Celery Stick*
- *Orange Slice*
- *Sherry*
- *Pineapple*
- *Flag (a cherry and an orange slice put together on a stick)*

Figure 7-22: Fruit Bar example

There are also more unusual garnishes, such as cucumber slices, kiwi, dill or other fruits and vegetables.

Sometimes, the type of garnish can influence the name of a cocktail. For example, a Martini ordered with onions (actually pearl onions) instead of the traditional olives, changes the name to a Martini Gimlet. If the guest orders a Dirty Martini, the preparation dictates that some of the liquid in which the olives are stored should be added to the drink.

The different ways a garnish can be placed in the drink include:

- *Inside the drink.*
- *Sitting on the top of the drink, when the texture allows it.*
- *Split on the rim of the glass.*

Notes:

5 | Wine Opening

This lesson you will learn how to:

- Open a bottle of red wine.

- Open a bottle of sparkling wine.

- Perform a white wine bottle opening service sequence.

LESSON FIVE

Wine Opening

Objectives

By the end of this lesson, you should be able to...

- State the three (3) major steps to follow when presenting any wine to a guest.

- Explain the three (3) items necessary to open a bottle of red wine.

- Explain and perform the difference between opening a bottle of red wine versus a bottle of sparkling wine.

- Perform white wine opening service, according to the standard demonstrated by the mentor.

Wine Opening

Overview of Opening Bottles

Even though there are thousands of different types of wines, there are but a few ways to open them. For a server, opening a bottle of wine is typically the first real "performance" that is "acted" for the table.

The more practiced you are at handling and opening bottles, the better impression you give guests. A server who is comfortable with opening wine bottles gives customers a good impression that can translate into satisfaction with the restaurant and its waitstaff's level of professionalism.

Opening a bottle of wine can be intimidating at first. But here are the guidelines to help you quickly look and feel like a pro.

We start after the customer has placed the wine order and you have it in your possession.

The procedure to follow for every wine is:

1. *Show the bottle to the guest who ordered it.*
2. *Clearly read the following information about the bottle:*
    ° The vintage of the wine.
    ° The name of the wine.
    ° Its classification, if any.
    ° The name of the producer (or land owner).
3. *Wait for the approval of the guest.*
4. *Open the bottle.*

For opening wines, there are generally three categories: white, red and sparkling.

The way to open each type is different.

Notes:

Red Wine

Generally, opening a bottle of red versus white wine are very similar. What makes red wine more difficult to open can be the age of the bottle and the condition of its cork. Sometimes a cork can become dry and brittle.

Be careful not to break the cork while removing it!

There are three items used to open a bottle of red wine:

1. *A wine key (corkscrew).*
2. *A napkin.*
3. *A small plate (B&B plate), optional.*

Figure 8-1: Equipment to open a bottle

Notes:

If you plan to open the bottle in front of the guest be sure to **stand the bottle on the table** while doing so. Not only is it easier, but it is safer! No one wants to spill wine on their customer.

The very first step to opening a bottle of red wine is to remove the foil. **Why?**
Because dirt and microorganisms can get under the foil and need to be cleaned off PRIOR to opening the bottle.

Be sure to cut away the foil far away from the cork, usually *below* the bulge at the top of the bottle. You may find it easier to simply remove the entire foil.

Figure 8-2: Cut the foil
below the bulge

Figure 8-3: Remove the foil

Wipe clean the entire top of the bottle. A damp napkin works best.

Twist the corkscrew into the center of the cork. Keep twisting straight down - *no pushing!*

Figure 8-4: Clean off the
bottle, including top

Figure 8-5: Insert and twist
down the corkscrew

Notes:

How can you tell if the corkscrew is far enough into the cork? The twisted part of the screw will be completely buried into the cork *and* the lever will fit comfortably on the bottle's top edge.

Place your finger to hold the lever and gently begin lifting the cork out of the bottle.

<u>Tip:</u> *Place your thumb on the bottle's side while lifting the corkscrew (see Figure 8-7).*

Figure 8-6: Place the level on the rim and hold

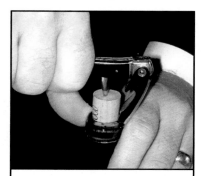

Figure 8-7: Remove the cork by lifting it

When the cork is almost out, bend it over a little to pull it out completely. It is okay to use your fingers, as seen in Figure 8-8 below.

Present the cork and foil (if the Sommelier or restaurant has this as a policy) to the customer - usually on a small plate.

Figure 8-8: Bend the cork slightly to remove quietly

Figure 8-9: Place the cork and foil on a small plate

Notes:

After the cork is out of the bottle, clean the opening. *Don't let any dirt fall into the bottle!*

The final step is to give the customer an opportunity to taste and approve the wine. Notice in Figure 8-11 how close the wine is to the cut foil.

Why it is so important to cut the foil away from where the wine could touch it?
If there are contaminants on the foil, the taste of the wine could be spoiled!

Figure 8-10: Clean off the bottle after the cork is out

Figure 8-11: Pour a taste

Wine can be poured into glasses with or without a napkin around the bottle.

Folding a napkin under the bottle allows the server to easily wipe away any drips from the neck of the bottle, like in Figure 8-12.

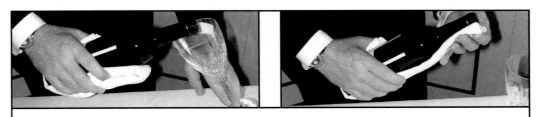

Figure 8-12: Wipe away any drips by using a napkin held under the bottle

Notes:

Sparkling Wine (Champagne)

Sparkling wines can come in a variety of bottle shapes and sizes.

Opening a sparkling wine, however, is the same no matter what size the bottle.

The most important thing about sparkling wine is to keep it cold. Bottles can be kept chilled in a variety of ways, the most traditional being a bucket filled with ice and water.

Do not overfill the bucket with water! Leave enough room to put in the bottle.

Quickly chill a bottle by placing salt (Kosher or Rock salt) in the bucket along with the ice /andwater.

Salt makes the ice melt faster and makes the water temperature colder (by lowering the freezing point of the water).

Figure 8-13: Sparkling wines come in a variety of sizes

Figure 8-14: Chill Sparkling wines

Do not hold the bottle by its neck, as this will warm the wine inside. To avoid warming the bottle's neck, hold it with a napkin.

After presenting the bottle to the customer, leave the bottle in the bucket to open it.

Notes:

There are only three steps to opening a sparkling bottle.

Step 1: Remove the foil. Most bottles have a ribbon on the foil that makes it easy to pull off the foil cap from the neck.

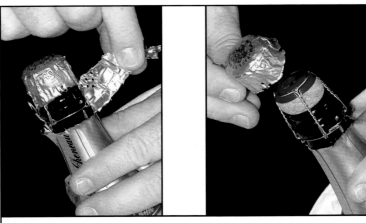

Figure 8-15: Remove the foil from the bottle - Step 1

Step 2: Remove the wire 'cage'. Pull out the wire buckle, found at the neck of the bottle and twist it five and a half times counterclockwise to loosen the cage. Carefully remove the cage and quickly add top pressure to prevent the cork from flying out accidentally.

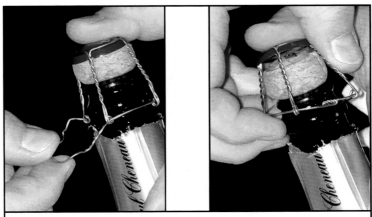

Figure 8-16: Remove the wire cage from the cork - Step 2

Notes:

Do not use the ice bucket as a garbage can to dispose of foils and corks.

Step 3: Remove the cork. This step is the most difficult, since it requires a little muscle and a lot of focus. *Slowly remove the cork by holding the bottle and twisting the cork.* When a cork is hard to pull out, put the bottle on the table, hold the cork very tight, and twist the bottle while holding the cork. It is just the opposite of the normal procedure, but it works!

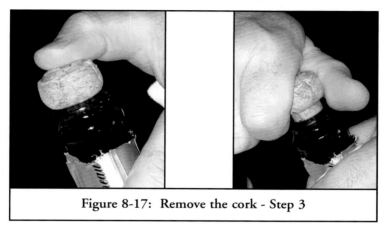

Figure 8-17: Remove the cork - Step 3

Be sure to keep your thumb on the cork until you are ready to remove it!

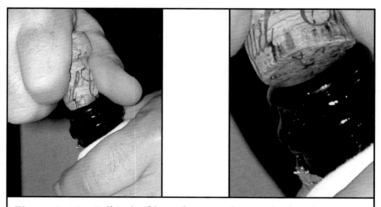

Figure 8-18: A 'hiss' of haze lets you know the bottle is open

A big "POP!" only wastes wine as it sends foam out of the bottle!

The goal is to remove the cork in such a way that only a "hiss" is heard as it's removed and only a haze of gas can be seen leaving the bottle (Figure 8-18).

Notes:

Figure 8-19: Pouring a Sparkling wine

How to Pour a Sparkling wine

When serving a regular size bottle at the table, a sparkling wine bottle should be held just like a bottle of red wine.

Sparkling wines have a indentation in the bottom of the bottle, called a 'punt'. Holding the bottle by underneath and with your thumb inside the "punt" of the bottle is only appropriate when pouring at a bar (because of the height of the bar) or when pouring magnum sized bottles

The way to pour for either a 'split' (half bottle) or regular size bottle is demonstrated in the series seen in Figure 8-19.

<u>Tip:</u> Pouring sparkling wine into a dry glass automatically fills that glass with foam.

At that point, the server can either wait for the foam to go down to finish pouring, or save time by filling all the table's glasses up with foam, then make a second round to finish filling them (this works the best for large parties).

Notes:

Wine Sequence of Service (White Wine Example)

The way to present wines is the same for all wines, whether they are white, red or sparkling. *The example below assumes that the following steps have been completed:*

1. An order for a white wine was taken.
2. The appropriate glasses were set in front of each guest.
3. The ice bucket was brought containing the wine, with a napkin covering it.

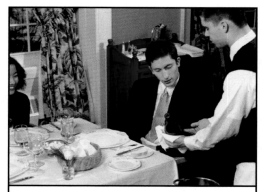

Figure 8-20: Show the bottle to
the customer for verification

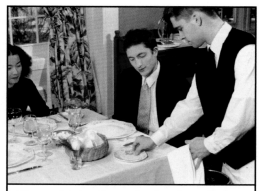

Figure 8-21: Open the bottle and place
the cork on the table

The bottle is brought to the guest who ordered it (seen in Figure 8-20), at the same time the server should:

1. *Show the bottle to the guest who ordered it.*
2. *Clearly read the following information about the bottle:*
   ° The vintage of the wine.
   ° The name of the wine.
   ° Its classification, if any.
   ° The name of the producer (or land owner).

Once approval is gained from the customer that this is, indeed, the correct selection - open the bottle.

Lay the cork / foil either on a small, B&B plate or directly on the table.

Notes:

Figure 8-22: Wipe the bottle

Figure 8-23: Pour a taste

Since wine is served chilled, the bottle is wiped after being removed from the ice bucket, as shown in Figure 8-22.

The guest who ordered the wine is then given a taste for approval (as shown in Figure 8-23).

Figure 8-24: Show the bottle to customer during tasting

Figure 8-25: Serve ladies first

As the guest tastes the wine, show the bottle to him (in Figure 8-24) so that he can look at it one more time before approving the wine be poured for the entire table.

After approval, the lady should be served first, as seen in Figure 8-25.

Notes:

Figure 8-26: Serve gentlemen next

Figure 8-27: Serve person who tasted last

Then the other gentlemen should be served, as in Figure 8-26.

Finally, the person who tasted the wine (most likely the host) is served (Figure 8-27).

Figure 8-28: Place bottle back
in the bucket

Figure 8-29: Take the cork away
from the table

To keep it cold, place the bottle back in the bucket and cover it with the napkin.

The plate that has the cork / foil is removed from the table (as in Figure 8-29), *unless the guest wants to keep the cork.*

Notes:

6 | Wine Essentials

This lesson reviews:

- **Wine Categories.**

- **Steps to Making Wine.**

- **Main Categories of Wine.**

- **Common Terms used by Wine Professionals.**

- **Food Pairing.**

LESSON SIX

Wine Essentials

Objectives

By the end of this lesson, you should be able to...

- Explain how wine labels differ depending on where they are grown or produced.

- List the four (4) conditions that impact how wine turns out.

- Explain the difference between Champagne and Sparkling wine.

- List the four (4) major categories of wine and give and example of each.

- Explain how wines get their color.

- Descibe the meaning of the 63 most common terms used to describe wine.

Wine Essentials

Organization of Wines

All wines are generally put into one of two categories:
Old World and New World

This does not necessarily refer to the way the wine is made, but the way it is referred to on the label. *In the United States, Chile and Australia, among other countries, wines are referred to by their varietal name. Examples include:* Kistler Chardonnay from California, Morandé Cabernet from Chile, and Peter Lehman Shiraz from Australia.

In places like France, Italy and Spain, you'll only find the names of the towns or vineyards on the bottles and that's about it.

<u>Here's why.</u> After centuries of trial and error, winemakers in Europe, mostly France, discovered which grapes grew best in a certain area. **These regions became identified with these grapes.** *So, if you saw a bottle of red wine from Burgundy, you knew it was Pinot Noir.* Certain towns or vineyards desiring to highlight the distinct characteristics - or "terroir" - of their wines only put the name of the town or the vineyards on the label.

The feeling is that it is not the grape that is important so much as where that grape is grown.

Winemakers from the New World are beginning to discover the importance of this type of identification by making it clear on the bottle where a particular wine came from.

However, most winemakers outside of Europe put the grape type (variety) name on the bottle.

This makes it much easier on the consumer, who may not know the difference between Gevrey-Chambertin and Hermitage. There are some well-known European exceptions who put the varietal names on the bottle. One example is Alsace, in northeastern France and Germany.

Notes:

Basic Principles of Winemaking

For 1000's of years, people have made wine out of just about any kind of fruit - not just grapes.

The two things required to make wine (otherwise known as vinification) are: sugar and yeast. For this book, we'll limit the discussion to wine made from grapes.
Four conditions impact the final outcome of the wine:

1. *The grape type;*

2. *Where the vines are grown and the variations in weather conditions;*

3. *What kind of soil the vines grow in;*

4. *And most importantly, the grape grower and winemaker (this is sometimes the same person). Decisions made in the field and in the winery have a great influence on the wine's quality, quantity, flavor, and aroma, among many other characteristics.*

The winemaking process begins once the grapes are harvested. *The wine grower measures the acidity, sugar levels of the grapes,* and the overall level of ripeness of the crop to make the final decision when to harvest. *The grapes can be gathered either manually or by machine.*

They are de-stemmed and repeated crushed to break the skin of the grapes. Pressing releases the juice from grapes. Sometimes yeast is added or the winemaker will rely on natural yeast found on the skin of the grapes to start the fermentation.

When yeast is introduced to sugar-laden juice, the yeast starts consuming the sugar. **The by-product of this process is carbon dioxide and alcohol.** As the yeast continues to consume the sugars, more CO_2 gas (which dissipates into the air) and alcohol is made. This process will continue until the yeast dies.

The yeast die when:

1. *All the sugars are consumed;*

2. *The alcohol content rises above 15%;*

3. *The temperature of the wine rises above 90 degrees Fahrenheit.*

The level of sweetness can be changed during the fermentation process by either stopping it or adding unfermented grape juice to the mix. Wines can be aged in barrels or stainless steel tanks after the desired level of fermenting is complete. Generally, wines are filtered for clarity.

Notes:

Red, White and Rosé Wines

Red wine does not result from merely squeezing red grapes. All grape juice is nearly the same color--a mostly clear, straw-colored liquid.

The color of red wine comes from the pigmentation (color) in the skin of red grapes. By leaving the grapes skins in with the juice, it takes on the color of the skin. The longer the skins are left with the juice, the more color the juice gets.

It is possible to make a white wine from red grapes. How? The pressed juice is separated from the skins as soon as possible.

In the case of white grapes, winemakers will sometimes leave the fermenting wine in contact with the skins for a period of time to let the flavor and yellow color infuse the juice. Rosé, pink or blush wines usually come from limited contacted with the skins prior to fermentation, although it is legal in most countries to blend in a little red wine into a white wine to achieve the desired color level.

Sparkling Wines

Certainly the most festive of all wines are those we call sparkling or bubbly wines. These are often incorrectly called Champagne. **Only the sparkling wine that comes from the Champagne region of France can truly be referred to as Champagne.**

As mentioned before, *the by-product of yeast-sugar reaction is alcohol and carbon dioxide.* When making still wine (wine without bubbles), the gas is released into the atmosphere. *When making sparkling wine, the CO_2 is trapped in the bottle.*

There are a number of ways to keep the gas inside the wine. The most common way (and the one that produces the highest quality product) is the méthode Champenoise. After a still wine is fermented, a yeast and sugar solution known as *"liqueur de tirage"* is put into the wine.

The wine is then placed in a tightly sealed bottle and preferably stored in a cool cellar or cave. **The *liqueur de tirage* causes a second fermentation inside the bottle, trapping the alcohol and carbon dioxide gas.**

Notes:

After about four weeks, the yeast die and the second fermentation process is complete.

Winemakers may choose to leave the now sparkling wine in contact with the dead yeast cells for a little or a long time. This creates the characteristic sparkling wine flavor known as toast.

After the yeast dies, there is the problem of removing it from the sparkling wine. **The famous Champagne house Veuve Clicquot developed a removal process in the 19th century that has more or less remained unchanged. It is called "riddling".** Every day the bottles are turned and shaken slightly to loosen any stuck yeast cells. The wine is stored in racks that hold the bottles by the neck. Each day the bottle is tipped a little higher to move the sediment down the bottle and finally in the tip near the cork.

Eventually, the bottles are nearly vertical in the rack, known as a pupitres. *Once the sediment has come to rest near the cork, the neck of the bottle is frozen.* The stopper is removed and the pressure in the bottle pushes out the ice chunk along with the ice-encased sediment. The bottles are topped off with little sparkling wine from another bottle. Sometimes a small amount of liquid sugar is added to give the wine its desired sweetness. The wine is then corked and labeled.

Aromatized Wines

Aromatized wines essentially are still wines that have flavors added to them. <u>*These wines, known as Vermouths,*</u> *typically come from areas that produce average quality bulk wines. Winemakers use herbs, spices, roots and bark to give the wine its desired flavor.* Aromatized wines come in red and white, sweet and dry.

Fortified Wines

Fortified wines are made by adding a neutral grain spirit or brandy to a still wine. *The spirit can be added to the wine before the fermentation process is finished to create sweet wine--as is the case with* **Port.** *Or the spirit can be added after the wine is made to create a dry wine--as is the case with* **Sherry** *(although some sherry makers add sugar later to create a sweeter versions).*

Besides sherry, which historically comes from Jerez, Spain, and Port, there are two other popular fortified wines: **Madeira** from the island of Madeira in Portugal, and
Marsala from the island of Sicily in Italy.

Notes:

Sauvignon

The Main Grapes

There are five different species of grape-bearing vines and hundreds of varieties of wine growing grapes. We will only address several of the most popular grapes used for wine production.

Whites

Chardonnay

The most well-known grape in the world, Chardonnay can be found in nearly every winegrowing region in the world. Its origins are hard to pin down, but like so many grape varieties it was first mastered in France. The most elegant and expensive Chardonnay comes from France's Burgundy region. **White Burgundy (all white wines from Burgundy are 100% Chardonnay) has also become most copied style of Chardonnay.** However, few winemakers outside of Burgundy have matched the buttery, spicy, lemony qualities found in the wines made in the towns of Meursault, Puligny-Montrachet and Chassagne-Montrachet.

The Burgundy style copied the world over is due to its use of oak barrels. The wine could use oak either during the fermentation process and/or while aging. Another style of Chardonnay somes from the Chablis area, which is northwest of the main Burgundy region. Here the wines are anything <u>but</u> buttery. They are fermented in stainless steel tanks and may or may not see any oak barrels during the aging process. **Chablis wines are best described as flinty and mineral-like with a crisp, clean acidity.** A few growing regions, including New Zealand, have chosen to copy this style of Chardonnay.

Riesling

One of the most desirable wines of the world. *Often associated with the vineyards of Germany, especially those along the Rhine and Mosel Rivers, Riesling is grown in many places throughout the world.* The grape enjoys a cooler climate and can be found in France's Alsace region, Australia, New York State, California and Washington State, where it is often called Johannisberg Riesling.

The image many people have of Riesling is that is always sweet and somewhat less desirable. **Being one of the most adaptable winemaking grapes, Riesling comes in every category from the very dry (no residual sugar) to very sweet (high percentage of residual sugar).**

Notes:

Sauvignon Blanc

Typically found in cooler wine growing areas, Sauvignon Blanc wine comes in more or less two styles. **There is the hay-like grass version.** These wines have the smell of fresh-cut grass and green plums.

The other is the melon style. You'll find this style of Sauvignon Blanc in the warmer climates and it will be a little more robust than the more acidic, refreshing grassy style. The melon style offers tastes of melons and apricots. **Often, this type of wine will spend a little or a lot of time in oak barrels, which gives it a creamy, vanilla aroma and taste.**

Sauvignon Blanc is grown the world over. *Some of the better regions producing this wine are Bordeaux and the Loire Valley in France, northeastern Italy, New Zealand, South Africa, Chile, Washington State and California.*

Pinot Gris

Growing in popularity, **Pinot Gris is often at its best when it is made in a light, crisp, acidic style.** *It has a mineral and lemon flavors and is an excellent companion to light fish dishes. It is especially enjoyable during hotter weather when it can be quite refreshing.*

Pinot Gris from France's Alsace region can be a bit more robust in flavor than most other Pinot Gris. In Alsace it is called Tokay d'Alsace Pinot Gris.

In addition to Alsace, you can find Pinot Gris in northeastern Italy, where it is called Pinot Grigio, Oregon and California.

Notes:

Reds

Cabernet Sauvignon

One of the most royal and one of the most common wines are the ones made with Cabernet Sauvignon. It can be blended in some of the finest and most expensive Bordeaux or used all by itself, such as those made in Napa Valley, California. It is also made in garden variety styles in just about every growing region in the world and comes in a wide range of prices.

The Cabernet Sauvignon grape is very small and has a thick skin. This translates into a high skin-to-juice ratio, which makes the wine taste very astringent or harsh. In addition, **Cabernet Sauvignon has naturally high acidity. In the right hands, a deep, dark powerful wine can be made out of these grapes.** In the hands of the less adept, the wines can be overwhelming and difficult to palate.

Many winemakers follow the lead of Bordeaux wineries and blend Cabernet Sauvignon with mellower wines, such as Merlot, to take off its rough edges. Australian winemakers have had particular success with blending Cabernet Sauvignon with Shiraz.

In addition to Bordeaux and Australia, excellent Cabernet Sauvignon and Cabernet Sauvignon-based wines can be found in Italy, Spain, Chile, California and Long Island, NY.

Merlot

Often very fruity with blackberry jam-like qualities, Merlot has grown in popularity in recent years, especially with those exploring red wine for the first time. It is a wine that is very easy to like since it is mellow, fruity and often not very complicated.

The classic home of Merlot is Bordeaux on the east bank of the Dordogne River in France.

Winemakers blend Merlot with Cabernet Sauvignon and other red varieties to give the simple Merlot-based wine more structure. In the United States, winemakers produce wines made of 100% Merlot, however many winemakers take a cue from Bordeaux and add a little Cabernet Sauvignon to give these jam-like, fruity wines a little more intensity and interesting flavors.

Winemakers in Chile, Italy, California and Washington State are capitalizing on Merlot's growing popularity.

Notes:

- Hardest to grow - food friendly/popular
- from burgundy - most expensive wine
- Grows well in Oregon
- Primary grapes in Champagne

Pinot Noir

One of the most difficult grapes to grow and to make into wine, Pinot Noir is one of the most popular and most food friendly wines in the world. Most wine lovers associate Pinot Noir with red wine from Burgundy, where they make wine from 100% Pinot Noir grapes. *Several of the highly prized vineyards in Burgundy produce some of the most expensive wines in the world.*

Other areas around the globe have had great success with Pinot Noir, especially winemakers in Oregon. *Despite being a red grape, Pinot Noir is one of the primary grapes used to make Champagne.*

Syrah/Shiraz

Syrah is one of the main grapes found in the steep river valleys of France's northern Rhône. **It is a full-bodied, spicy wine that also provides the drinker with delicious blackberry, black currant and plum characteristics.**

In the middle of the 19th century, Syrah was introduced to Australia, where it is known as Shiraz. Since then, it has become one of the most widely planted grapes in the country. Australian winemakers produce a variety of styles from low-quality jug wines to wines of great international renown, such as the famous Grange Hermitage. They have also had great success blending Shiraz with varieties such as Cabernet Sauvignon, Merlot and Grenache.

You can also find Syrah (or Sirah as it is sometimes spelled) in California and Italy.

Zinfandel

Once thought to be related to the Primitivo grape of southern Italy, researchers have traced the origins of the Zinfandel grape back to Croatia's Crljenak grape.

Regardless of its scientific geneology, **American vintners claim Zinfandel as the only "true" winemaking grape in North America.** *Historically known for making big, fruity, zesty wines that are often high in alcohol, most people now associate Zinfandel with the blush (or rosé) version known as white Zinfandel.*

In addition to the hotter California wine growing regions, winemakers cultivate this grape in Brazil and South Africa.

Notes:

Common Terms

Acidic
A term to describe a wine tartness. It can indicate unfavorable characteristics when there is excess acid in the wine.

Appearance
The way a wine looks, which can range from "crystalline" to "cloudy". Some wines appear dark as ink while others watery. A cloudy appearance may indicate a wine is unfiltered or perhaps has problems due to age or improper storage.

Amarone
Italian for "strongly bitter". This is a process of winemaking classically found in the Veneto region of Italy. The grape bunches are harvested and left on racks for several months. This allows the moisture in the grapes to evaporate leaving behind a nectar that is high in sugar. These grapes are then pressed and fermented. If the process is stopped before the wine is completely fermented, the wine is known as recioto. If fermentation is allowed to convert all the sugar to alcohol, the wine becomes an amorone. Amarone wines are known for their relatively high alcohol content.

Appassimento
Appassire in Italian means "to dry" or "to wither". Thus, appassimento is the process of making wine in the Valpolicella, Italy, from partially raisinated grapes, a holdover from the days when man first learned to preserve fruit by drying it.

Approved viticultural area (AVA)
A growing region defined by the Bureau of Alcohol, Tobacco and Firearms, the federal agency that governs the production of wine in the United States.

Appellation Contrôlée
French wine law that spells out specific growing regions, wine label information and growing, harvesting and fermentation criteria.

Appellation d'origine Contrôlée
The highest category of quality wines under French wine law. AOC producers must follow strict guidelines for growing, harvesting and fermenting grapes and the subsequent labeling. Among other rules, AOC rules specify vineyards, districts, towns and regions where certain grapes can be grown.

Notes:

Balance
When all the taste components - acids, tannins, fruit, among others - work harmoniously together, the wine is considered in balance. When one of these components overpowers the others, the wine is considered out of balance.

Barrel aging
After wines are fermented, they are often placed in oak barrels to receive the tastes from the wood and to soften some of the harsh characteristics of young wines.

Barrel fermentation
The process of fermenting wines in small casks, usually made of oak, instead of large stainless steel or wooden tanks. While more expensive and less controllable than steel tanks, the procedure gives the wine a creaminess and subtle oak flair. Barrel fermentation is usually reserved for white wines, such as Chardonnay and Sauvignon Blanc.

Big
A term used to describe full-bodied, rich wines.

Blanc de noirs
Literally "white of black" in French, this term indicates a white or blush wine made from red grapes. It is typically reserved for sparkling wines made from the Pinot Noir and Pinot Meunier. It is occasionally used for still blush wines made from red grapes.

Blanc de blancs
Literally "white of white" in French, this term indicates a white wine made entirely from white grapes. It is typically only said for sparkling wines made from 100% Chardonnay grapes. Blanc de blanc wines are usually light and delicate.

Body
The perceived weight of wine, which is actually a combination of alcohol, extract, glycerol and acid. A full-bodied wine displays rich, complex, powerful characteristics. A light-bodied wines are generally more simple and lack the powerful tastes of a full-bodied wine. Medium-bodied wines are in the middle. Light-bodied wine does not mean low quality. A great light- or medium-body wine may offer finesse and other refined characteristics.

Notes:

Bordeaux, Bordeaux-style wines

A red wine (unless otherwise indicated as a white Bordeaux or a sweet Bordeaux) that is a blend of two or more of the following grape varietals: Cabernet Sauvignon, Merlot, Cabernet Franc, Petit Verdot and Malbec. To a lesser extent, winemakers may also use Gross Verdot, Carmenere and St. Macaire. A white Bordeaux blend could include Sauvignon Blanc, Mucadelle and Sémillon.

Bouquet

Often confused with aroma, bouquet refers to the complex fragrances that develop as a wine ages in a bottle.

Botrytis cinerea

Also known as noble rot, pourriture nobile (France), Edelfäule (Germany) and Muffa nobile (Italy), *this mold attacks grapes draining them of moisture but leaving behind a highly concentrated nectar found in many dessert wines.* This disease occurs only in certain environmental conditions.

Breathing

Exposing the wine to air prior to drinking. While some disagree, people who believe in letting wine "breath" or "aerate" say it softens the tannins in younger red wines and allows complex bouquets to develop in older wines. Generally, lower quality reds, white wine and very old wine do not benefit and may diminish from their exposure to air.

Burgundy

A winemaking region south of Dijon France known for making some of the world's best Pinot Noir and Chardonnay wines. Winemakers in the United States have used the term generically to mean red wine.

Brut

A term applied to the driest of sparkling wines. That is they contain very little residual sugar. Extra brut indicates a wine that is extremely or totally dry.

Notes:

Cava

Spanish term for sparkling wine. These wine typically come from Spain's northern winemaking regions and must be made using the méthode champenoise.

Chablis

The northernmost region of Burgundy, France, known for outstanding Chardonnay wines. Winemakers in the United States have used the term generically to mean a white wine.

Champagne

A region in France known for its sparkling wines. Winemakers in the United States have used the term generically to mean sparkling wine.

Corked

A descriptor that indicates the wine has been tainted by a chemical compound called 246 tri-cloroanisol or 246-TCA. This chemical is found in some corks and can be detected by humans at extremely low levels, as little as 30 parts per trillion. The chemical gives wine a musty taste of wet cardboard or damp newspapers.

Decanting

Decanting either separates wine from particulates and sediment deposited during the aging process or to soften assertive young wines. It can also be done with most any wine to show the server's skill and add flair to a guest's dining experience.

Dry

A wine without any residual sugar is considered dry. During the fermentation process, yeast turns sugars found in the grape juice into alcohol and carbon dioxide gas.

If these sugars are completely consumed, the wine is considered dry. If a noticeable amount of sugar is left in the wine, it is considered off-dry.

Notes:

Earthy
A wine tasting term used to describe tastes or aromas usually associated with damp soil.

Edelfäule
See botrytis cinerea.

Enophile
Lover of wine.

Finish
The final impression left from a taste of wine. A lingering, distinctive "finish" speaks well for a wine. A short or lacking finish signals a lower quality wine.

Grand cru
The French phrase for "great growth" has slightly different meanings throughout France. In essence, *grand cru indicates grapes were grown in ideal or special locals,* which could be an area of a vineyard, a district containing several vineyards, or a designation given to a particular wine producer.

Green
Most often, green refers to a wine that is too young to drink. However, green can be used to describe wine made from under-ripe grapes. These wines often are quite high in acid but lack in fruit flavor.

Hot
A wine tasting term used to describe wines high in alcohol.
Overly hot wines give a burning sensation in the throat and mouth and are considered *out of balance.*

Legs
The wine "tears" found on the inside of a glass after swirling the wine. The presence of legs usually indicates a wine is rich and full-bodied.

Notes:

Meritage
A Bordeaux-style wine that is usually red. See Bordeaux.

Méthode Champenoise
A process of making sparkling wine in which a finished still wine has yeast and sugar added to it and is then rebottled. This "dosage", as it is called, creates a second fermentation in the wine. As with any fermentation, the sugars are converted to alcohol and carbon dioxide by the yeast. Since the fermentation takes place in a closed bottle, the CO_2 gas is absorbed into the wine. It is this absorbed gas that gives sparkling wines their bubbles or sparkle. Once the second fermentation is complete, the dead yeast cells are removed through a process of riddling (regularly turning the bottles as they sit topside down in racks so the sediment settles at the opening of the bottle) and disgorging (chilling the bottles to reduce the pressure in the bottle, thus allowing the sediment to be gently pushed out). The final pressure in a standard bottle of sparkling wine can range from 60 to 90 pounds per square inch. Caution should always be used when opening sparkling wines.

Muffa nobile
See Botrytis Cinerea.

Musky
Term used to describe a wine that presents earthy characteristics.

Noble Rot
See botrytis cinerea.

Oxidized
Term generally used to describe a wine that has decayed due to either poor storage (often overheated) or exposed to air by accident. Often noticeable at sight by a change of the color of the wine to a light brown color, the taste veers to a light nutty and sherry like flavor.

Oxygenation
See "Breathing"

Off-dry
See "Dry".

Notes:

Passed
A wine that has passed its maturity level and is starting to degrade.

Port, Porto
A sweet fortified wine typically served after the meal. Port comes in several varieties including vintage, ruby and tawny. Tawny ports are lighter in color and have a brown sugar and raisin taste. The other ports are deep red to brown with a fruitier taste. Vintage ports, which can age 50 years or more, have a good deal of sediment and must be decanted. Porto indicates the wine is shipped from the city of Oporto, Portugal, the classic home of this wine.

Punt
Indentation in the bottom of a wine or sparkling wine bottle. The punt give the bottle more structural integrity and also serves to catch sediment.

Rhône
An arrid wine growing region along the Rhône river in southern France known for Syrahs, Viognier and many other grapes.

Ripasso
The addition of juice from select Valpolicella grapes to the pomace leftover from the fermentation of Amarone. When the young wine from the previous year's harvest is added to the rich, wine-soaked skins, a second process of fermentation is encouraged which imparts color, tannin, fruit and alcohol to the mix. The resulting wine still possesses some of the fresh character of classic Valpolicella, but also exhibits additional complexity and richness very similar to Amarone.

Pomace
Leftover from the grapes after they were pressed to extract the juice. This residue can potentially be used further to make brandy.

Sekt
Term used for sparkling wine in Germany and other German-speaking areas. True German sekt is usually fruity and little sweeter than its counterparts in France, Spain, Italy and the United States.

Notes:

Smoky
Tasting term used to describe the smoke-like qualities in a wine's aroma and taste. It is something akin to a light campfire or flint smoke.

Soft
A term used to describe a wine that is mellow and without the harshness normally associated with tannin and acid. Soft implies good balance.

Sur lie
French for "on the lees". Lees is the sediment left over after fermentation. It can contain dead yeast cells, grape skins, grape pits, particles of vine and grape leaves.

Winemakers leave their wine sur lie to increase complexity and improve flavor in a wine. Sparkling wines made in the méthode champenoise necessarily are left on the lees because yeast is added to the wine after it has been put into the bottle. Wines that that have been made sur lie generally gain a creamy, yeasty, fresh bread quality.

Terroir
A French word meaning the entire environment encompassing the vineyard, including the soil, subsoil, weather conditions and its position in relation to the Sun.

Texture
An impression of weight that a wine gives when it is on the palate (or mouth). It derives from a wine's glycerin among other factors, which make the wine seem thicker than water. Wines lacking or absent of texture are referred to as thin or watery.

Toasty
A term used to describe toasted bread characteristics in a wine's aroma or taste. Toasty characteristics are often found in sparkling wines and in some Chardonnays.

Trocken
German for "dry".

Notes:

Ullage
Air space created in the top of barrels and bottles due to evaporation. Ullage in older wines may be a product of the natural aging process. Ullage in younger wines generally indicates a problem with the cork.

Unbalanced
When one or more of a wine's taste components-acids, tannins, fruit, among others-dominates over the others, the wine is considered unbalanced.

Unctuous
A descriptor used for a wine that is extremely sweet, rich and has a heavy, almost oily texture.

Vanilla
A descriptor used for wines with a vanilla-like aroma or taste. Vanilla qualities usually come from time spent by a wine in an oak barrel during and/or after fermentation. Some winemakers also use oak chips and extracts to achieve the tastes and smells of vanilla.

Vin de pays
French for "wine of the country". It is the third lowest quality level for French wines, just above the lowest quality level, vin de table. Producers of vin de pays enjoy fewer restrictions and are allowed higher grape yields than the two highest quality levels, vin délimité de qualité supérieure and appellation d'origine contrôlée, which is the highest level of quality. Vin de pays should not be confused with vin du pays, which means local wine and has no legal meaning.

Vitis vinifera
A species of grapevine that is most commonly associated with winemaking. It is native to Europe as well as East and Central Asia, but has been planted worldwide.

Yeasty
A descriptor used for wines that have spent time sur lie, which means on the dead yeast and grape sediment after fermentation is finished. Yeasty can be best described as having tastes and aromas of fresh bread or bread dough. While desirable in sparkling wines and certain white wines, it is considered a flaw in most wines.

Notes:

Food and Wine Pairing

Much has been written about food and wine pairing. For practical purposes here, the best guide would be to keep it simple. There is no definitive theory on matching wine to food, but a couple of simple concepts should allow you to make competent selections when a guest, chef or event planner calls you on to pick a wine.

Power with Power

The first rule of thumb is to match power with power. *What we mean when we say match power with power is that wine, like food, has a certain power level or intensity?* Think about a nice, crisp Sauvignon Blanc from the Sancerre region in France. This is a light, fresh, fruity wine. It's fair to say that this is not a powerful wine.

Now, think of a thick Moroccan lamb stew with garlic mashed potatoes and grilled vegetables. Is "light" the first word that comes to mind when you think of this dish? No, this is a heavy, meaty dish. Not only is the meat rich and fatty, the preparation has lots of spices and the sauce is thick and heavy. This dish ranks high on the power scale. So, the Sancerre is probably not a good choice based on the power with power guideline.

Competent food wine pairing also means knowing which wines not to recommend. The lamb dish would overwhelm even the most powerful white wine. This eliminates all whites and indeed many lighter reds, such as Beaujolais, most Pinot Noirs, most Chiantis and many Rioja wines. This dish calls for something along the lines of a Cabernet Sauvignon, Syrah or spicy red Zinfandel to match the intensity of flavors in the lamb dish.

Complement or Contrast

*Once you understand the power with power rule, there are really **no wrong choices** from this point on, just matters of opinion.* The next step in food and wine pairing is deciding whether to complement or contrast the flavors in the dish.

<u>*Let's use another example.*</u> Your guest orders a grilled salmon with a lemon-dill butter sauce. Salmon is pretty fatty and rich. The same can be said for the sauce. You can go one of two ways here. It really depends upon the situation and what you want to do.

Notes:

Do you want to emphasize the richness of this dish? In other words, do you want to mimic the charcoal flavors of this fish and the butteriness of the sauce? If you said yes, then you would be advocating a complementary wine. Let's choose a big, creamy Chardonnay, like the ones often made in California, Australia and Chile. These would be decadent, indulgent choices of wine. And that's OK provided the situation calls for it.

Why do we use terms like indulgent and luxurious to describe this suggestion? It might be best to think about the interaction of flavors going on in one's mouth. You take bite of the fish after swirling it around in the sauce. You taste the butter in the sauce and the fatty fish flavors and then there's that yummy charcoal spiciness left over. You take a sip of wine. Lo and behold, you taste nearly the same things. There's the creaminess that comes from the time the wine spent in oak barrels. After you swallow you're left with the unmistakable taste of cloves and nutmeg spices. Each bite and sip builds on the previous bite and sip.

When would this type of complementing suggestion be appropriate? That's hard to say. It may come down to personalities of those drinking it. You may want to think of the reason for the meal. Is it a birthday, anniversary or some other kind of celebration? This would be a time for less restraint in the meal. The wine pairing should reflect that indulgent attitude.

Now, let's consider contrasting. Take the same dish, but pair it with a Chablis, an unoaked Chardonnay from New Zealand or a crisp, lemony Muscadet from the Loire Valley, France. The highlight of these wines is their acid, which tastes like the refreshing sensation you find in a green apple or some tropical fruits.

Let's again take a bite of salmon, but we then take sip of the Chablis, which lacks the creaminess and spiciness of the first wine. The crispness of the wine and the bracing acidity cleanses your mouth of the heavy, buttery, creamy sensations coating the inside of your mouth. It puts you back to where you were before you took a bite.

Personal preferences should again dictate on whether the contrasting wine is suggested. But also consider the situation. Perhaps this is a business lunch or maybe the guests are dining outside in the early summer. Can you see how you might show some restraint with the choice of wine?

Notes:

Advanced Pairing

Can food and wine pairing be more complicated? *Obviously it can.* There are many great books written on this subject, in fact. There may be specific flavors in the food that can be highlighted with certain wines. You may also want to emphasize regional characteristics of the food and wine, choucroute with a crisp, fruity Alsatian Riesling for example.

At this level of pairing, however, you must become more familiar with the unique tastes of wine varietals and how winemakers, vintages and regions influence them. You must also become aware of the different food tastes and preparations. These and other factors can play important role in the selection of the wine, but expertise in food and wine pairing comes with time and experience.

Notes:

7 | Common Sense Rules Certification Test

In this lesson you will be taught:

- **Common sense rules about dining etiquette according to the IBGS hospitality guidelines (International Business & Gourmet Standard of Hospitality).**

- **Understand the process to achieve and maintain FDRP Certification.**

LESSON SEVEN

Common Sense Rules / Certification Testing

Objectives

By the end of this lesson, you should be able to...

- List at least three (3) generally unacceptable, yet unwritten, restaurant rules.

- Describe the process to receive FDRP Certification with 100% accuracy.

Common Sense Rules

These are common sense rules that are accepted by the vast majority of restaurants regardless of their style or standing. They set a very good standard and philosophy of work.

It Is Generally Not Appropriate To...

...**Offer anything complimentary to a guest without consulting the Maitre D', his assistant or the management.** The reason for this is that there are ways to complement the guests with items in a way that instill in the guest a certain respect for the professionalism of the establishment. There is more into it than just to "comp" stuff.

...**Find excuses.** *Regardless of what is happening, the responsibility of a dining room professional is to **deal with problems, not to walk away from them**.* Once upon a time a server went to tell a large party that the reason that they were waiting so long for their main course was that V.I.P. guests were "dining in another room and the kitchen is taking care of their table first." That statement cost that establishment $1,983.73 in 1997. The non-V.I.P. guests were executives that generated a lot of repeat business to this establishment. The Food and Beverage Director had to "comp" the entire meal the next day to rebuild the relationship. When in doubt, get the Maitre D' or his assistant's opinion on what to say.

...**Justify yourself.** "The kitchen is backed up" is not going to make the guest like you. You only look like you are walking away from your responsibilities, which could anger guests.

...**Use professional terms with guests.** The guests should be addressed in a professional manner in terms they understand. "Welcome to R-room" (when referring to the Rothschild room), "Front of the house" or "I am sorry but the veal is 86" are professional slang phrases. AVOID THEM when speaking to your guests.

...**Speak to guests in affectionate terms, such as "folks," "guys," "fellaz," or "how are we doing?"** *Speak to guests as if they have a great impact on your life. Speak to them courteously and respectfully. Don't infringe on their comfort zone by becoming too familiar or casual with them.* Address guests as Ladies and Gentlemen or Sir and Madam, or Ma'am, even in casual restaurants.

It Definitely Is Not OK To…

… **Make up answers.** For example, if a customer dines alone and asks if he can order a bottle of wine and take whatever he can't finish with him, check with the Maitre D' or his assistant to make sure that it is possible. *Do not assume you know the local alcohol laws.* In some states, you may unintentionally break the law.

… **Talk to a guest when they are eating, even if they are trying to talk to you.** If guests have food in front of them, excuse yourself and walk away.

…. **Use abusive or profane language.**

… **Take partial orders.** If guests tell you that they want to order their appetizers and wait to order their main course until they get their first course, tell them that this is not possible. Realize that if they later order a medium-well rack of lamb, they might be waiting 40 minutes for it. If you have an insistent guest, call for the Maitre D' or his assistant.

… **Agree to split any dish without thinking first.** Don't ask the kitchen to split a "Poached egg with caviar," when it's obvious that it is not possible to split a soft egg and keep its presentation.

… **Discuss gratuity with a customer.** Management may use the amount/percentage of gratuity left by the customer as a gauge to evaluate how the customer perceived the quality of service. If the gratuity is unusually low, management may decide to inquire further with the customer how their service was (without mentioning the gratuity) to attempt to learn if anything negative happened, and try to gain the opportunity to correct it.

In no circumstances a waiter should discuss gratuity with a customer, with the exception that when a gratuity is unusually high AND if management gives permission to the waiter to discreetly thank the customer for his/her generosity.

You Should Be Aware That...

...**The timing can make or break a meal** when it relates to firing of food. You are empowered with the responsibility to identify guests that eat unusually fast or slow, to warn the kitchen so they can act by speeding-up or slowing-down the preparation of the food for that table.

...**Offer cracked pepper may change the balance of flavors in a dish.** There is somebody in the kitchen who has worked very hard to come up with a perfectly balanced dressing and who has handpicked different greens to balance their bitterness. Have some respect for the cooks in the kitchen! It would be a shame to spoil a dressing trying to look good, and it is telling the guests that the kitchen can't finish their plates right on their own.

...**If you identify a guest with special needs, you can address the management.**

...**If you have concerns about guest's** language/behavior, address the management.

...**To check identification for any individual that looks under 30 years old is not an option,** but an obligation. Your personal liability, not the restaurant's, is at stake.

...**You are responsible, as a dining room professional, for your station set up from A to Z.** This includes the cleanliness of the station as well as team member's uniform presentations.

...**If you have guests with special requests,** address your need to the Maitre D'/Manager.

...**Professionals speak and act without prejudice** to age, disability, gender, race, religion, ethnic origin, sexual orientation or veteran status.

...**Chocolate and after dinner mints** are not to be served with the check, but with the coffee. Chocolate compliments coffee better than paper.

...**In the United States, people drink coffee WITH their dessert.** Very often coffee is actually served while guests are waiting for dessert. Offer coffee when taking the dessert order. Only offer coffee prior to dessert if there is a delay in obtaining the dessert cart for presentation to the table.

...**You can tell management the straight story when you face an issue.** For example, if you spilled a tray of Champagne glasses onto a gentleman's back, simply say "I spilled a tray of Champagne glasses on position 1, Table 33." It is not a big deal. Professional management will handle it, and will show you how to interact with the customer and your future staff.

...**A guest does not need to be under medical constraint** to have a special food request accommodated.

You Should Also Be Aware That...

...Once the guest has completed the transaction, the check should be taken away. The following benefits are gained by removing the check prior to the guest's departure:
- The server can verify that the card slip is properly signed.
- The server can ensure that the guest did not mistakenly take both credit card receipts with them.

...When presenting a check, it is considered inappropriate for the server to hand a check to a guest and hold it until they take it directly when they obviously are not ready to do so or do not wish to give attention to the check presentation. The waiter should just leave the check.

...If you are educated in the matter of dining and etiquette, this knowledge and experience should be put to use for the service of the guests, not against it.

...In a dining room, very few things actually ARE a big deal if you react well to them. The big deal is HOW you deal with them.

...Nothing you do for a guest should be perceived as a big deal, even if you have to do something extraordinary for them.

...YOU are why this industry is great, or bad.

...There is no other profession on earth, besides teaching, where a person has so much opportunity to enrich another person's life.

True Professionals...

...Demonstrate and adhere to ethical business practices, with due respect for all.

...Promote understanding and respect for those beverages used in the hospitality industry and refrain from abuse of drugs and alcohol.

...Treat all equipment and property as if it were personal property.

...Extend a polite and courteous manner to all visitors and colleagues.

...Stay open-minded to the opinions of others; work with a positive attitude.

...Share knowledge with others.

...Are reliable and dependable.

...Act with honesty and integrity with all people.

...Come on time for their appointments.

Certification Test

Certification Testing Overview

Individuals who study the material covered in this manual are prepared to take the *Certified Dining Room Associate (DRA)*™ and/or the *Certified Associate Wine Steward (WSA)*™ tests. There are two ways to take these tests: 1) Use the Federation's Web Testing Center, or 2) Use hard-copy printed tests.

How to take the Test Online

This page may or may not include a unique Examination Code(s). For those books without codes included, one can be purchased through the FDRP online store, at www.FDRP.com, or by calling us 904/491-6690. FDRP provides the following overview information on the certification testing process.

1. Access the Internet through your service provider.
2. Place the following address in the address-bar of the browser window: *www.FrontSUMMIT.com*
3A. IF you do not have a personal account yet setup on FrontSUMMIT® create an account by clicking on [*New User*]
   a) If you were provided a "*Site Code*" by your organization, type it in the appropriate field.
   b) If you are taking certification as an independent individual and you are not embedded in an educational institution or organization that needs to monitor your certification, enter "*fdrp1*" in the "*Site Code*" field.
3B. IF you already have a personal account setup on FrontSUMMIT® access your account by typing your "*Username*", "*Password*" and "*Site Code*" in the login box.
4. Scroll down to the bottom of your account page and enter the following codes in the designated fields:

DRA examination code	WSA examination code
JWUCDRATLYY8644	HUSTCAWSECUP3328

5. You may then access the tests by clicking on the desired test icon.
6. At the end of the test your results are immediately displayed. If you scored the minimum required to succeed (80% correct), a certificate link will appear next to your test link on you account page.
7. You may use the certificate link to bring the certificate up for printing and documenting your credential.

Note: Each respondent's test result is automatically logged at the Federation's headquarters.
You may obtain a professionally printed certificate with a gold-foil seal, as well as a certification lapel pin from FDRP.

How to take a Hard Copy Test Report

The double-sided page printed at the back of each Associate Handbook (seen to the right) is called an **FDRP Test Report**. For those individuals who are taking the test using this document, it is very important to properly fill out each section and sign (both the instructor and the student), then mail to the FDRP Certification Department. Educators must gather all student tests and send them as a group to:

FDRP, Certification Dept - 1417 Sadler Road, #100 - Fernandina Beach, FL 32034 USA

FDRP recommends that educators make copies of each Test Report prior to sending them, and mail to the FDRP office in a delivery method that reduces the chance of loss. We, unfortunately, do not accept faxed copies of *Test Reports*.
For hard-copy testing, please allow up to twenty-one (21) days to process the certification.

Certified Dining Room Associate (DRA)™
FDRP TEST REPORT
Code of Conduct, Professional Ethic and Pledge of Hospitality

The FDRP makes available numerous certification designations for individuals to convert their training, education and experience into valuable credentials. FDRP certified individuals at every level become ambassadors of the Federation and are expected to:

… Demonstrate & adhere to ethical business practices, with due respect for customers and colleagues.
… Promote understanding and respect for beverages used in the hospitality industry and refrain from the abuse of drugs and alcohol.
… Treat all equipment and property as if it were personal property.
… Extend a polite and courteous manner to all visitors and colleagues.
… Stay open-minded to the opinions of others; work with a positive attitude.
… Share knowledge with others.
… Be reliable and dependable.
… Act with honesty and integrity in their interactions with all people.
… Be punctual for their appointments.

The FDRP requires that you make the following pledge:
I acknowledge that following my certification by the Federation, I pledge to uphold the standards of hospitality and conduct presented in the FDRP certification manual, and will place the interest of my clients above my own. I agree to hold the FDRP and its Judge Panel harmless from any and all liability in the event my certification would be rejected on the basis of information provided to theFDRP by me or third persons which would, in the judgment of the FDRP, make me ineligible for certification or is grounds, in the judgment of the FDRP, for my certification to be revoked. I agree to accept the Judge Panel's decision as to my eligibility for certification and maintaining certification. I have read and understood the FDRP Standards of Certification (located on the Web Testing Center).

Date:_____ / _____ / _____ Signature: _____

Student Name: | | | | | | | | | | | | | | | | | | | | | | | | | | | | | | |

(please print exactly as it should be printed on the certification card)

Educator Acknowledgement, Student Certification Endorsement

I, undersigned, certify that the written examination was administered according to the FDRP requirements:

1. 25 minutes time limit from distribution to collection of their examination sheet;
2. Closed book test;
3. Students were not provided any assistance and were not allowed to help each-other.

I further acknowledge that the practical examinations and standards of performance graded on the back of this sheet are accurate and were evaluated as per the measurable criterion defined in my *Instructor Toolkit* for each of the required standards.

Educator Name: _____ _____
(Please print)   (Signature)

Business Name: _____ Class ID: _____

This student has a FrontSUMMIT account: ☐NO ☐YES:_____
(Print STUDENT *FrontSUMMIT* USERNAME)

If this student HAS NOT a FrontSUMMIT account: FDRP must create an account for the student under the educator's account using the educator's SiteCode:_____
(Print EDUCATOR *FrontSUMMIT* SITECODE)

MAIL TO: FDRP, Certification Dept; 1417 Sadler Road, Fernandina Beach, FL 32034, USA.

Educator to Complete This Portion for *Dining Room Associate (DRA)*

Toolkit code ....

Test number DRA-V11-...

I attest that the student whose name appears on this application can perform the following tasks as per the rating below without any assistance.

	Very Well	Comfortably	Partially	Not at all
Load, carry and unload three (3) plates by hand.	☐	☐	☐	☐
Load, carry and unload a bar tray with beverages, and a bussing tray with plates and other utensils.	☐	☐	☐	☐
Set a table, given a specific set up style for a given menu.	☐	☐	☐	☐
Perform American Service.	☐	☐	☐	☐
Perform the most common methods of water, bread & butter service.	☐	☐	☐	☐
Clear at least three (3) main course set ups.	☐	☐	☐	☐
Perform red and sparkling wines opening.	☐	☐	☐	☐
Present/clear menus and take a F&B order with 100% accuracy.	☐	☐	☐	☐

Student to Complete This Portion

DRA examination code* ....

■ Yes   ▨ ⊠ ☑ *Not acceptable*

Mark answers filling in the entire box. Unanswered questions are considered incorrect.

Question 1 ☐☐☐☐☐ A B C D E True ☐ ☐ False
Question 2 ☐☐☐☐☐ A B C D E True ☐ ☐ False
Question 3 ☐☐☐☐☐ A B C D E True ☐ ☐ False
Question 4 ☐☐☐☐☐ A B C D E True ☐ ☐ False
Question 5 ☐☐☐☐☐ A B C D E True ☐ ☐ False

Question 6 ☐☐☐☐☐ A B C D E True ☐ ☐ False
Question 7 ☐☐☐☐☐ A B C D E True ☐ ☐ False
Question 8 ☐☐☐☐☐ A B C D E True ☐ ☐ False
Question 9 ☐☐☐☐☐ A B C D E True ☐ ☐ False
Question 10 ☐☐☐☐☐ A B C D E True ☐ ☐ False

Question 11 ☐☐☐☐☐ A B C D E True ☐ ☐ False
Question 12 ☐☐☐☐☐ A B C D E True ☐ ☐ False
Question 13 ☐☐☐☐☐ A B C D E True ☐ ☐ False
Question 14 ☐☐☐☐☐ A B C D E True ☐ ☐ False
Question 15 ☐☐☐☐☐ A B C D E True ☐ ☐ False

Question 16 ☐☐☐☐☐ A B C D E True ☐ ☐ False
Question 17 ☐☐☐☐☐ A B C D E True ☐ ☐ False
Question 18 ☐☐☐☐☐ A B C D E True ☐ ☐ False
Question 19 ☐☐☐☐☐ A B C D E True ☐ ☐ False
Question 20 ☐☐☐☐☐ A B C D E True ☐ ☐ False

FDRP & AHE & AHC Use Only: Pass/Fail
*report DRA code from page 152

PRACTICAL EXAM POSITIVE RESULTS		
REQUIRED	RECORDED	P / F
5		

PRACTICAL EXAM POSITIVE RESULTS		
REQUIRED	RECORDED	P / F
16		

Certified Associate Wine Steward (WSA)™
FDRP TEST REPORT
Code of Conduct, Professional Ethic and Pledge of Hospitality

The FDRP makes available numerous certification designations for individuals to convert their training, education and experience into valuable credentials. FDRP certified individuals at every level become ambassadors of the Federation and are expected to:

… Demonstrate & adhere to ethical business practices, with due respect for customers and colleagues.
… Promote understanding and respect for beverages used in the hospitality industry and refrain from the abuse of drugs and alcohol.
… Treat all equipment and property as if it were personal property.
… Extend a polite and courteous manner to all visitors and colleagues.
… Stay open-minded to the opinions of others; work with a positive attitude.
… Share knowledge with others.
… Be reliable and dependable.
… Act with honesty and integrity in their interactions with all people.
… Be punctual for their appointments.

The FDRP requires that you make the following pledge:
I acknowledge that following my certification by the Federation, I pledge to uphold the standards of hospitality and conduct presented in the FDRP certification manual, and will place the interest of my clients above my own. I agree to hold the FDRP and its Judge Panel harmless from any and all liability in the event my certification would be rejected on the basis of information provided to theFDRP by me or third persons which would, in the judgment of the FDRP, make me ineligible for certification or is grounds, in the judgment of the FDRP, for my certification to be revoked. I agree to accept the Judge Panel's decision as to my eligibility for certification and maintaining certification. I have read and understood the FDRP Standards of Certification (located on the Web Testing Center).

Date:_____/_____/_____ **Signature:** _____

Student Name: | | | | | | | | | | | | | | | | | | | | | | | | | | | | | | | |
(please print exactly as it should be printed on the certification card)

Educator Acknowledgement, Student Certification Endorsement

I, undersigned, certify that the written examination was administered according to the FDRP requirements:
  1. 25 minutes time limit from distribution to collection of their examination sheet;
  2. Closed book test;
  3. Students were not provided any assistance and were not allowed to help each-other.
I further acknowledge that the practical examinations and standards of performance graded on the back of this sheet are accurate and were evaluated as per the measurable criterion defined in my *Instructor Toolkit* for each of the required standards.

Educator Name: _____ _____
(Please print)   (Signature)

Business Name: _____ **Class ID:** _____

This student has a FrontSUMMIT account: ☐ NO ☐ YES:_____
(Print STUDENT *FrontSUMMIT* USERNAME)

If this student HAS NOT a FrontSUMMIT account: FDRP must create an account for the student under the educator's account using the educator's SiteCode:_____
(Print EDUCATOR *FrontSUMMIT* SITECODE)

MAIL TO: FDRP, Certification Dept; 1417 Sadler Road, Fernandina Beach, FL 32034, USA.

Educator to Complete This Portion for *Associate Wine Steward (WSA)*

Toolkit code ....

Test number WSA-V11-.................................

I attest that the student whose name appears on this application can perform the following tasks as per the rating below without any assistance.

	Very Well	Comfortably	Partially	Not at all
■ Perform red wine opening.	☐	☐	☐	☐
■ Perform white wine opening from a wine bucket.	☐	☐	☐	☐
■ Perform sparkling wine opening.	☐	☐	☐	☐
■ Perform red wine & sparkling service for a table of four.	☐	☐	☐	☐
■ Perform wine service according to rules of precedence.	☐	☐	☐	☐
■ Perform proper wine glasses handling without using a tray.	☐	☐	☐	☐
■ Load, carry and unload beverages from a bar tray.	☐	☐	☐	☐
■ Present/clear a wine list and record a wine order with 100% accuracy.	☐	☐	☐	☐

Student to Complete This Portion

WSA examination code* ....

■ Yes   ▨ ☒ ☑ *Not acceptable*

Mark answers filling in the entire box. Unanswered questions are considered incorrect.

Question 1
☐ ☐ ☐ ☐ ☐ ☐ ☐ ☐
A B C D E F G H
☐ ☐ ☐ ☐ ☐
I J K True False

Question 2
☐ ☐ ☐ ☐ ☐ ☐ ☐ ☐
A B C D E F G H
☐ ☐ ☐ ☐ ☐
I J K True False

Question 3
☐ ☐ ☐ ☐ ☐ ☐ ☐ ☐
A B C D E F G H
☐ ☐ ☐ ☐ ☐
I J K True False

Question 4
☐ ☐ ☐ ☐ ☐ ☐ ☐ ☐
A B C D E F G H
☐ ☐ ☐ ☐ ☐
I J K True False

Question 5
☐ ☐ ☐ ☐ ☐ ☐ ☐ ☐
A B C D E F G H
☐ ☐ ☐ ☐ ☐
I J K True False

Question 6
☐ ☐ ☐ ☐ ☐ ☐ ☐ ☐
A B C D E F G H
☐ ☐ ☐ ☐ ☐
I J K True False

Question 7
☐ ☐ ☐ ☐ ☐ ☐ ☐ ☐
A B C D E F G H
☐ ☐ ☐ ☐ ☐
I J K True False

Question 8
☐ ☐ ☐ ☐ ☐ ☐ ☐ ☐
A B C D E F G H
☐ ☐ ☐ ☐ ☐
I J K True False

Question 9
☐ ☐ ☐ ☐ ☐ ☐ ☐ ☐
A B C D E F G H
☐ ☐ ☐ ☐ ☐
I J K True False

Question 10
☐ ☐ ☐ ☐ ☐ ☐ ☐ ☐
A B C D E F G H
☐ ☐ ☐ ☐ ☐
I J K True False

Question 11
☐ ☐ ☐ ☐ ☐ ☐ ☐ ☐
A B C D E F G H
☐ ☐ ☐ ☐ ☐
I J K True False

Question 12
☐ ☐ ☐ ☐ ☐ ☐ ☐ ☐
A B C D E F G H
☐ ☐ ☐ ☐ ☐
I J K True False

Question 13
☐ ☐ ☐ ☐ ☐ ☐ ☐ ☐
A B C D E F G H
☐ ☐ ☐ ☐ ☐
I J K True False

Question 14
☐ ☐ ☐ ☐ ☐ ☐ ☐ ☐
A B C D E F G H
☐ ☐ ☐ ☐ ☐
I J K True False

Question 15
☐ ☐ ☐ ☐ ☐ ☐ ☐ ☐
A B C D E F G H
☐ ☐ ☐ ☐ ☐
I J K True False

Question 16
☐ ☐ ☐ ☐ ☐ ☐ ☐ ☐
A B C D E F G H
☐ ☐ ☐ ☐ ☐
I J K True False

Question 17
☐ ☐ ☐ ☐ ☐ ☐ ☐ ☐
A B C D E F G H
☐ ☐ ☐ ☐ ☐
I J K True False

Question 18
☐ ☐ ☐ ☐ ☐ ☐ ☐ ☐
A B C D E F G H
☐ ☐ ☐ ☐ ☐
I J K True False

Question 19
☐ ☐ ☐ ☐ ☐ ☐ ☐ ☐
A B C D E F G H
☐ ☐ ☐ ☐ ☐
I J K True False

Question 20
☐ ☐ ☐ ☐ ☐ ☐ ☐ ☐
A B C D E F G H
☐ ☐ ☐ ☐ ☐
I J K True False

FDRP & AHE & AHC Use Only: Pass / Fail
*report WSA code from page 152

PRACTICAL EXAM POSITIVE RESULTS		
REQUIRED	RECORDED	P / F
5		

PRACTICAL EXAM POSITIVE RESULTS		
REQUIRED	RECORDED	P / F
16		

Congratulations on your *Certification* as an *Associate!*

This achievement entitles you to **WEAR** a **DRA/WSA Pin** displaying your credential

Certification Pin ORDER FORM

Please send me the DRA/WSA certification pin!

Name (first / last)   Date Certified   Mentor Name   WSA DRA

.... / .... / .... ☐ ☐

Certification was achieved under the tutelage of [school name / establishment name] (if applicable),

....

Campus / Establishment Location (City / State) / Faculty Name

....

Billing Address:

 Name: ....

 Number/Street/Apt or Suite #: ....

 City: ....State/Country: ....Zip: ....

 Telephone: ....e-mail: ....

Mailing Address (if different from billing):

 Name: ....

 Number/Street/Apt or Suite #: ....

 City: ....State/Country: ....Zip: ....

10.00^{(1)}$ + S&H$^{(2)}$; Member price: $8.00 Membership #$^{(3)}$ _____ - _____

CA PIN $	....
+ S&H$^{(2)}$	7.50
Total $	....

(1) All amounts are charged in US Dollars
(2) $7.50 continental US; Outside US call + 1 (904) 491 6690
(3) Please place membership number in order to benefit from the 'Member price'

Name as printed on card   *Cardholder Signature*

METHOD OF PAYMENT   **CREDIT CARD ACCOUNT NUMBER** **EXPIRATION** **ALPHA CODE** $^{(4)}$

☐ ☐ **VISA** ☐ **MasterCard** ☐☐☐☐ ☐☐☐☐ ☐☐☐☐ ☐☐☐☐ ☐☐ ☐☐ ☐☐☐☐

            (4) The 4 digit number printed on front of credit card, right and above the engraved card number

Certified Associate Wine Stewards & Certified Dining Room Associates

Help Us To Know You

How many years have you worked in the hospitality industry? ....

Do you plan on seeking further certification? ☐ Yes ☐ No ☐ Not sure

Do you wish to receive more information about FDRP? ☐ Yes ☐ No ☐ Later

  If you answered 'yes', tell us how you would like to be contacted (phone, e-mail, address):

  ....

  If you answered 'Later' to this question, tell us when you would like to be contacted:

  ....

Comments ....

....

Fax Transmital Form - Fax to: + 1 904.491.6689

67050397R00095

Made in the USA
Lexington, KY
31 August 2017